HOME SECURITY

THE ENCHANTED WORLD
LIBRARY OF NATIONS
HOME REPAIR AND IMPROVEMENT
CLASSICS OF EXPLORATION
PLANET EARTH
PEOPLES OF THE WILD
THE EPIC OF FLIGHT
THE SEAFARERS
WORLD WAR II
THE GOOD COOK
THE TIME-LIFE ENCYCLOPAEDIA OF GARDENING
THE GREAT CITIES
THE OLD WEST
THE WORLD'S WILD PLACES
THE EMERGENCE OF MAN
LIFE LIBRARY OF PHOTOGRAPHY
TIME-LIFE LIBRARY OF ART
GREAT AGES OF MAN
LIFE SCIENCE LIBRARY
LIFE NATURE LIBRARY
THE TIME-LIFE BOOK OF BOATING
TECHNIQUES OF PHOTOGRAPHY
LIFE AT WAR
LIFE GOES TO THE MOVIES
BEST OF LIFE
LIFE IN SPACE

This volume is part of a series offering home owners detailed instructions on repairs, construction and improvements which they can undertake themselves.

HOME REPAIR
AND IMPROVEMENT

HOME SECURITY

BY THE EDITORS OF
TIME-LIFE BOOKS

TIME-LIFE BOOKS
AMSTERDAM

TIME-LIFE BOOKS

EUROPEAN EDITOR: Kit van Tulleken
Assistant European Editor: Gillian Moore
Design Director: Ed Skyner
Photography Director: Pamela Marke
Chief of Research: Vanessa Kramer
Chief Sub-Editor: Ilse Gray

HOME REPAIR AND IMPROVEMENT

EDITORIAL STAFF FOR HOME SECURITY
Editor: William Frankel
Assistant Editor: Lee Hassig
Designer: Kenneth E. Hancock
Picture Editor: Adrian Allen
Text Editors: Russell Adams Jr., Richard Flanagan,
Bob Menaker, Mark Steele, David Thiemann
Staff Writers: Lynn Addison, Megan Barnett, Stephen
Brown, Alan Epstein, Steven J. Forbis, Geoffrey
Henning, Leslie Marshall, Brooke Stoddard, William
Worsley
Art Associates: George Bell, Lorraine Rivard, Richard
Whiting
Editorial Assistant: Susanne S. Trice

EUROPEAN EDITION
Series Director: Jackie Matthews
Text Editor: Charles Boyle
Researchers: Louise Egerton, Caroline Manyon
Writers: Chris Farman, Fergus Fleming
Designer: Linda McVinnie
Sub-Editors: Jane Hawker, Hilary Hockman

EDITORIAL PRODUCTION
Co-ordinator: Nikki Allen
Assistant: Maureen Kelly
Editorial Department: Theresa John, Debra Lelliott

THE CONSULTANTS: Garry Barrs served a five-year apprenticeship as a locksmith before starting his own security business in 1982. His company specializes in fitting and servicing security locks and intruder alarm devices.

Doug Jones formerly designed and installed fire detection systems. He is now responsible for the design and installation of intruder alarm systems.

Leslie Stokes was a self-employed carpenter and joiner for seven years, specializing in purpose-made joinery and internal fittings. Since 1976 he has taught in the building department at the Hammersmith and West London College.

Alan Bayliss served his apprenticeship with a leading Sydney cabinet-making firm. He worked as a carpenter and cabinet-maker for 18 years, then took a teaching diploma from Sydney College of Advanced Education. Since 1970 he has been a teacher of cabinet-making at Sydney Technical College.

Contents

1 Barriers Against Break-Ins 7

A Chain-Link Fence at the Property Line 8

Low-Cost Security Lights for the House and Garden 14

Corrective Surgery for Vulnerable Doorways 18

Barring the Door: the Basic Locks and Bolts 22

Putting On a Better Lock 26

Securing Windows Against Forced Entry 38

Safes and Vaults: Fortresses Within the House 40

The Techniques for Welding Steel Grilles 46

2 Silent Sentries, Loud Alarms 57

Choosing a Simple but Effective Warning System 58

Where to Put Smoke Detectors 61

A Network of Protection From a Central System 62

How Electronic Alarms Work: Two Basic Circuits 64

How to Snake Cables Through the House 66

Sensors: the Eyes and Ears That Detect Trouble 72

Controls and Switches to Bypass Sensors 82

Protecting Your Car and its Contents 86

3 Defences Against Fire 89

Easy Ways to Make Your House Hard to Burn 90

Walls and Floors to Contain a Blaze 92

Putting Out a Small Fire With a Hand Extinguisher 97

Safe Exits From an Upstairs Window 99

What to Do if Fire Breaks Out 100

4 Coping With Everyday Hazards 103

Easy-to-Build Fences to Make a Garden Safe 104

Defusing the Dangers of Bathrooms and Stairs 108

Keeping Knives and Poisons Out of Reach 116

Adapting a House to the Needs of the Infirm 118

Credits and Acknowledgements 124

Index/Glossary 125

1 Barriers Against Break-Ins

A welded metal joint. In a brilliant shower of sparks, an electric current arcs between a white-hot electrode and two steel bars that form part of a custom-made grille. Both electrode and steel are melted to create a welded bead as rigid as the bars. The grille will be bolted or mortared into the masonry surrounding a window to form an impregnable defence against break-ins *(page 54)*.

Statistics explain why security has become a major concern for almost everyone. Since World War II, the burglary rate has been rising steadily in cities, suburbs and rural areas. Between 1979 and 1984, the amount paid out by British insurers to compensate for household theft rose from £48 million to over £200 million a year. There are no longer any "safe" areas. In London, every householder now has a one in 13 chance of being burgled each year, and in Sydney and other major cities throughout the world, the figures are comparable. Public concern is reflected in the ever-increasing amount of money spent on high-security locks and other sophisticated anti-burglar devices.

Fire *(pages 89–101)*, however, is more of a danger to personal safety than burglary: over 50,000 home fires occur in the United Kingdom each year, killing some 800 people. Even more threatening than fire are household accidents *(pages 103–123)*, which kill more than 5,000 people and injure more than 1,500,000 seriously enough for them to require hospital treatment. Some 500 people a year die from poisoning alone—deaths that could be considerably reduced if medicines were kept safely out of the hands of children *(pages 116–117)*. A safe and secure home requires protection against all these hazards. An alarm system should warn of fires as well as burglary; a fence may be needed not so much to keep an intruder out as to keep a toddler or pet in; and locks on external doors should be both burglar-proof and also, in case of an emergency, simple to open from the inside.

But burglary remains a principal concern, largely because most homes, even if newly built, are poorly equipped to bar intrusion. It is still rare to find a new home fitted with a mortise deadlock on all its exterior doors. Simple improvements—a fence that is difficult to scale *(pages 8–13)*, locks for doors and windows that cannot be jemmied *(pages 22–39)*, several strategically placed outside lights *(pages 14–17)*—can persuade would-be burglars to try their luck elsewhere. How elaborate you make your defences depends on your evaluation of the risk, based on your own experience and that of your friends and acquaintances. Burglary is a lesser threat in a suburban street, where friendly neighbours are often around to keep an eye on things, than in an impersonal block of flats or a remote cottage.

Every measure you take involves compromises, even when you follow professional advice. The police, for instance, often recommend barred windows and double-locked doors, yet fire-prevention officers prefer entrances that can be opened easily for quick rescues. The common-sense choices described on the following pages can give your family the reasonable protection they need, simply and economically.

A Chain-Link Fence at the Property Line

Any fence defining your property line is a psychological barrier to illegal entry, but a high chain-link fence is a formidable physical obstacle as well. Difficult to scale, it slows or prevents entry altogether, but what is more important to a potential burglar, it severely hampers exit, making removal of valuables awkward even for an athletic criminal and exposing him to view.

Chain link is not only effective; it is also inexpensive and easily installed. Two workers can erect 90 to 150 metres of fencing, complete with gates, in a matter of days. The lightweight wire mesh requires support posts spaced no more than 3 metres apart. Straining posts fitted with diagonal struts are set at the corners of the fence and at any other sharp bend. The posts should be embedded in concrete for maximum strength.

The strongest and most expensive type of chain-link fencing, galvanized to prevent rust, weathers to a dull grey. At less cost, you can buy mesh with a coloured vinyl coating over thinner, ungalvanized steel; dark green is popular because it blends with shrubbery to make the fencing virtually invisible.

Where you can place a fence and how high it can be is sometimes governed by local regulations. Many private properties have covenants concerning the nature of boundary divisions. Regardless of law, it is wise to agree the boundary lines with neighbours. An error that causes the fence to infringe on a neighbour's property is embarrassing and could prove costly.

Before ordering materials, draw a rough map of fence lines to scale. Mark locations for intermediate—or line—posts and for the stronger straining posts needed at ends, gates and corners and at the tops and bottoms of slopes of more than 1 in 4. Using the map, a fence supplier can equip you with wire mesh, posts and hardware for the job. Many suppliers also hire out special tools, such as fence pliers, cutters for mesh, and post-hole diggers.

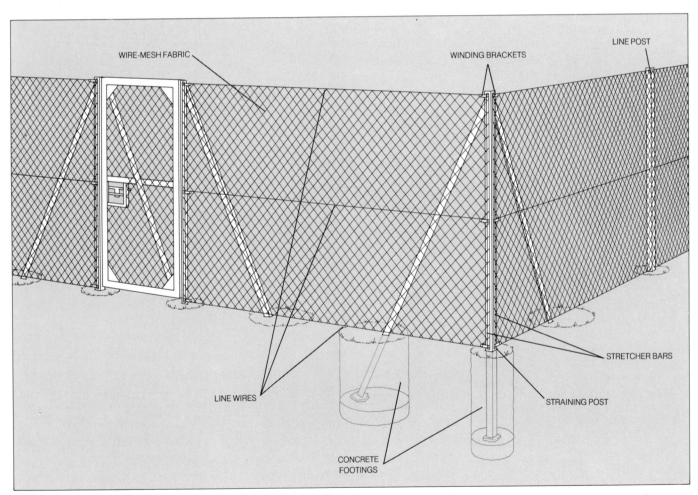

WIRE-MESH FABRIC

WINDING BRACKETS

LINE POST

STRETCHER BARS

STRAINING POST

LINE WIRES

CONCRETE FOOTINGS

Anatomy of a chain-link fence. Every component of this fence is prefabricated. Straining posts strengthened with diagonal struts at corners, ends and gateways, and the lighter line posts between straining posts, set 600 mm deep in concrete footings, hold the wire mesh. Line wires, running through the line posts and secured to straining posts with winding brackets, provide lateral support. Metal stretcher bars, slipped through links of mesh and secured to the winding brackets, tighten the mesh during installation. Wire ties attach mesh to line wires.

Setting up the Posts

1 Marking the post holes. Drive stakes to mark the locations of corner, gate and end straining posts, and get a helper to mark the height of the fence down from the tops of the posts. String a line between the corner and end stakes and mark off equal segments of 3 metres or less, driving in stakes to mark the intermediate line post holes.

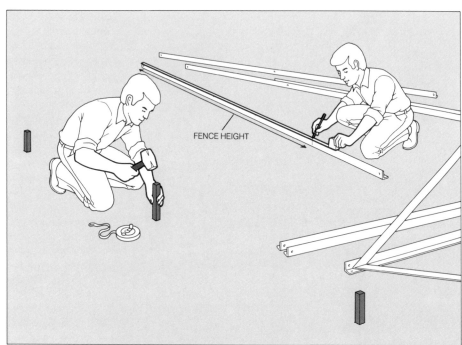

FENCE HEIGHT

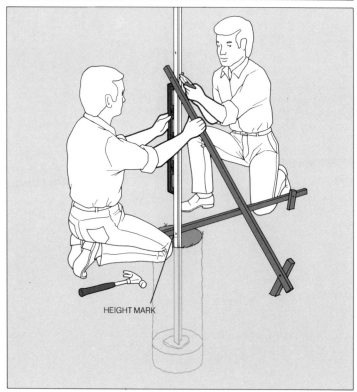

HEIGHT MARK

2 Digging the holes. Remove the stakes and, using a post-hole digger or a spade, dig holes for line and straining posts. Make the holes about 300 mm in diameter and deep enough to take a quarter of the length of the posts plus about 100 mm; holes for the diagonal struts of straining posts should be 600 mm wide. Line the bottom of each hole with a 100 mm layer of concrete using a stiff mix: 2½ parts cement, 3 parts sand, 5 parts gravel and 1¼ parts water. If you encounter a large immoveable stone at a depth greater than 300 mm, shorten the posts and use the stone as a base instead of concrete. For stones that lie closer to the surface, move the post hole to one side.

Where the property slopes more than 1 in 4 between gates or corners, dig holes for extra straining posts at the top and bottom of each slope.

3 Bracing a post plumb. Drive two stakes on adjacent sides of the post hole. Hammer a long nail through one end of two 50 by 25 mm bracing boards and fasten the other ends to each stake with a single nail. Set a post in the hole, centred over a flat stone at the bottom, and check that the mark made in Step 1 is at ground level. Use a spirit level to plumb a side of the post adjacent to a bracing board. When that side is plumb, bend the nails in the upper end of the bracing boards round the post. Brace all the posts except gateposts.

4 Setting a post in concrete. Check the braced post for plumb, then fill the hole with a stiff concrete mix *(page 9, Step 2)*. Overfill the hole slightly and use a trowel to bevel the concrete down from the post for runoff. Within 20 minutes, re-check the post for plumb and make small adjustments, adding more concrete as necessary. Set all the posts except the gateposts. Allow the concrete to set for at least 24 hours before removing the braces or attaching fencing.

5 Aligning the gateposts. Insert the hanging post into its hole. While a helper holds the hanging post plumb, hang the gate on the spindles and let it swing. The gate should not scrape the ground when it is opened; if it does, change the flat stone in the post hole for a slightly thicker one. Brace the post and set it in concrete following the instructions for Steps 3 and 4. When the concrete has set, stand the slamming post in its hole. Make sure that it is plumb, then close the gate to check that the latch is at the correct height *(right)*. Brace and concrete the post in position.

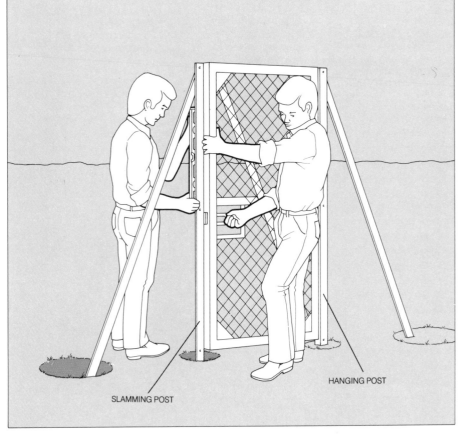

SLAMMING POST

HANGING POST

Fitting the Wire Mesh

1 **Attaching the winding brackets.** Using spanners to tighten the bolts, attach winding brackets to each of the straining posts. For any fence more than 1.2 metres high, fit six brackets to each straining post: one at the top, one at the bottom and one midway on each face. For a lower fence it is necessary to fit two pairs only, one at the top and one at the bottom.

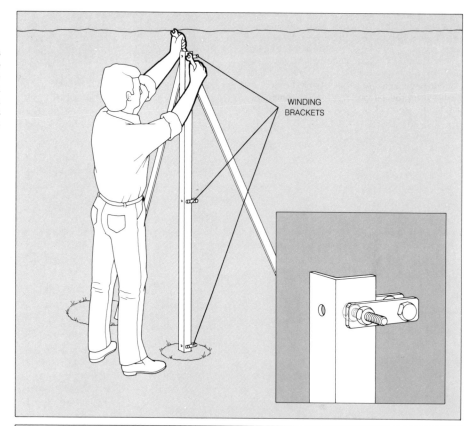

WINDING
BRACKETS

2 **Straining the line wire.** Unroll the wire and cut it to lengths that fit between the straining posts, allowing an extra 300 mm. Slot one end of a length of wire through the hole in the winder of one of the brackets and tighten the winder up a few turns with a spanner. Pass the wire through the corresponding holes in the intermediate line posts to the next straining post and attach it to the winder. Turn the winder until the wire is fully taut. Repeat this process between the straining posts to produce the wire frame on which to hang the mesh. Make sure that you have tightened all the winding brackets to their full extent.

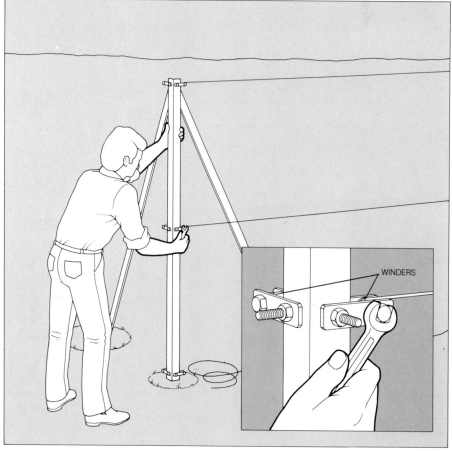

WINDERS

3 **Fixing the stretcher bar.** Stand the roll of mesh on its end and weave a stretcher bar through the first row of links. With nuts, attach the stretcher bar on to the protruding bolt threads of the winding brackets on one face of a straining post, as shown on the right.

If you are installing the fence on a slope, get a helper to hold the mesh while you weave the stretcher bar so that it remains parallel to the straining post *(inset)*.

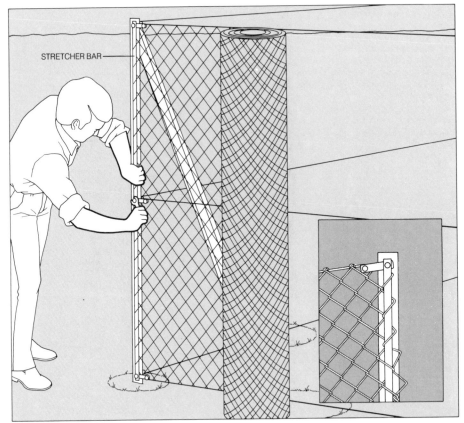

STRETCHER BAR

4 **Attaching the mesh.** Unroll the mesh along the line wires to the nearest straining post and fix it to the top wire with temporary ties. Weave a stretcher bar through a row of links just short of the straining post and, while a helper pulls the mesh taut, secure the stretcher bar level with the post *(above)*, secure the bar to the post. Cut off the excess mesh, twisting the strands of each severed link together with pliers and bending them back over the stretcher bar before moving on to the next section. Keep the mesh taut throughout this process.

Finally, secure the wire mesh to the line wires with wire ties. Set them 150 mm apart on the top wire, and 450 mm apart on the two lower wires, twisting them tight with pliers *(inset)*.

Double Gates for Driveways

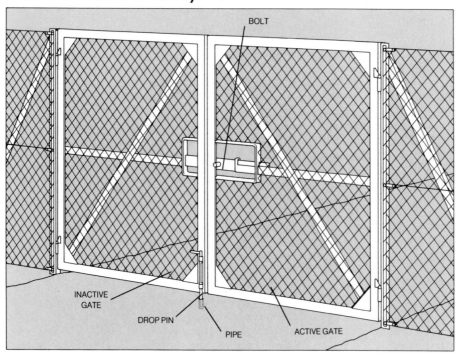

Installing the gate. Fit a double gate the same way as a single gate *(page 10, Step 5)*; close the gate and offer up the latch before concreting in the second post. When both gates have been hung, close them and slide the bolt to keep them closed. Loosen the drop pin on the inactive gate and let it fall to the ground. Mark its location. In a concrete or asphalt surface, use a masonry bit to drill a hole for the pin; in dirt or gravel, drive in a pipe 12 mm wider than the pin to act as a stop.

How to Make a Splice

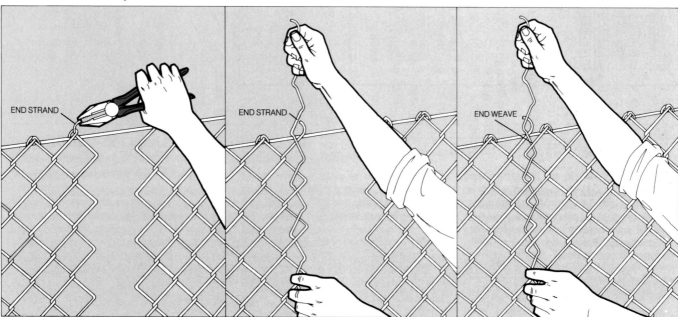

Weaving the wire. When you come to the end of the first roll of wire mesh, hoist alongside it one end of a fresh roll and, using pliers, loosen the top and bottom wires of the end strand *(above, left)*. Pull the strand from the wire weave by screwing it corkscrew-fashion out of the mesh *(above, centre)*. Pull the ends of the two rolls of wire mesh together, and weave the strand back down through the end weaves of both rolls *(above, right)* to join them together.

Low-Cost Security Lights for the House and Garden

Night prowlers tend to avoid a lighted house and garden rather than risk being noticed by neighbours or passers-by. The light does not have to be strong—an artificial equivalent of bright moonlight will do. Nor does it have to be stark and forbidding. Indeed, a lighting system can add to the appearance of a house, creating a welcoming atmosphere for both residents and visitors.

There are several factors to bear in mind when planning your system: the size of the area to be lit, the cost of installation, the efficiency and life span of the lamps and the quality of light they give out. The efficiency of a lamp depends on how much light it gives out for each unit of power consumed: this measurement is expressed as lumens per watt.

Incandescent lamps, also used for most indoor lighting, are the cheapest to install. Moreover, they give out a warm white light that is attractive as well as protective. On the other hand, they emit only 12 lumens per watt and have a life span of little more than 1,000 hours. A slightly more expensive form of incandescent lighting is tungsten halogen, with lamps emitting around 20 lumens per watt and lasting for up to 1,500 hours.

Mercury vapour lamps are another option. Although more expensive than tungsten halogen lamps, they are also more efficient, emitting 35 lumens per watt and lasting for up to 12,000 hours. Avoid the standard lamps, which give off a harsh, bluish light better suited to an industrial estate than a back garden. Instead, go for the colour-corrected lamps, which give a softer, more balanced light.

Fluorescent lamps are also worth considering. Traditionally, these were large, unwieldy and glaring. But more compact units are now available, and as well as being easier to install than the normal tube-type lamp fittings, they also produce a softer light. Although they cost less than mercury vapour lamps, fluorescents are just as efficient, emitting some 55 lumens per watt and lasting for up to 9,000 hours.

Near the top of the price scale are low-pressure sodium lamps, which emit up to 170 lumens per watt and last for up to 8,000 hours. These figures are impressive, but they have to be set against the fact that low-pressure sodium gives off a lurid yellow light which does little to enhance its surroundings. Most expensive of all, but also most efficient, are the high-pressure sodium lamps, emitting up to 120 lumens per watt and lasting for up to 20,000 hours. Unlike the low-pressure models, they give off a warm, golden light that will suit almost any domestic environment.

Whichever type of lighting you choose, you need to make sure that it comes on at dusk and goes off at dawn. The answer is to install a photocell—a light-operated switch that will automatically turn the lamps on and off as necessary. You can buy each light with its own built-in photocell, or you can buy a separate photocell and use it to control all the lights. The advantage of the second arrangement is that it is cheaper than the first; the disadvantage is that, if the photocell fails, all the lights fail too. It is safer, therefore, to install one or two lights with integral photocells and link the rest to a single unit. Either way, each light should still be provided with a manual control switch, otherwise you will have to carry out any checking at night. If the light comes with an integral photocell, it will need its own switch; if it shares a photocell, it will need a shared switch.

Deciding where to place the lights is as important as selecting the right type. There are three main options: you can place the lights on the house itself, mounting them on the walls or directly under the eaves; you can place the lights away from the house, fixing them on the ground or mounting them on trees, poles or specially designed lampposts; or you can place some lights on the house and some away from it, as illustrated on the opposite page, above. The choice will depend upon the size and layout of your particular property, as well as your own personal taste.

Remember, though, that the purpose of security lights is not to turn your garden into an airport runway, but simply to get rid of any shadows that might provide cover for an intruder. Remember, too, that where the lamp is placed away from the house, you will need to install either an underground or overhead supply cable. Unless you are experienced at this type of work, you should leave it to a qualified electrician. The same consideration also applies where an outside wall lamp is being connected to a separate photocell.

However, where the lamp comes with an integral photocell, installation should be fairly straightforward *(pages 16–17)*. It will generally be possible to run the new cables—one from the lamp, and one from the manual control switch—to an existing lighting circuit via a joint box.

As for the box itself, this is best placed in the attic, where you should be able to reach the wiring of the lights below without pulling up carpets or floorboards. Another advantage of fixing the joint box in the attic is that you can drill the hole for the supply cable through a soffit board, which is much easier than drilling through a wall.

You should make sure that all electrical work complies with the Regulations for Electrical Installation, published by the Institution of Electrical Engineers. Not legally binding, the Regulations constitute the basic code on electrical safety and standards for the U.K. In Australia and New Zealand, all electrical work must be carried out by a qualified practitioner.

A sample lighting system. Few houses have exactly the same layout and security lighting requirements as the example shown in the drawing below, but the principles illustrated here can be applied to almost any house and garden. The high-pressure sodium spotlight mounted on the ground lights up the far end of the garden path and most of the tree. High-pressure sodium wall lights, mounted at the top of the front and back of the house, illuminate the doors and windows. The garage at the right of the building is covered by an incandescent spotlight mounted under the eaves. A street lamp illuminates the entire area to the left of the house, and so no new fixtures are needed there.

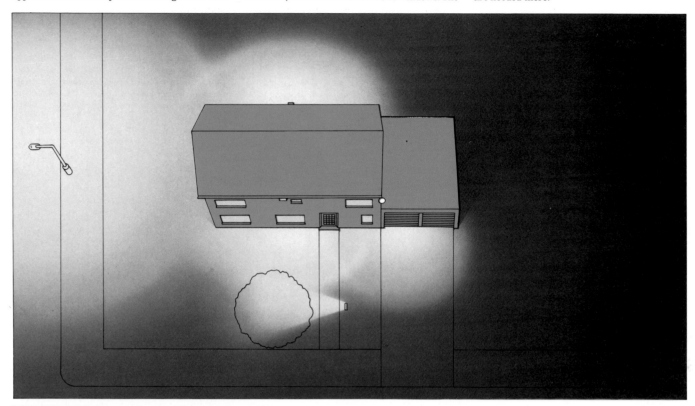

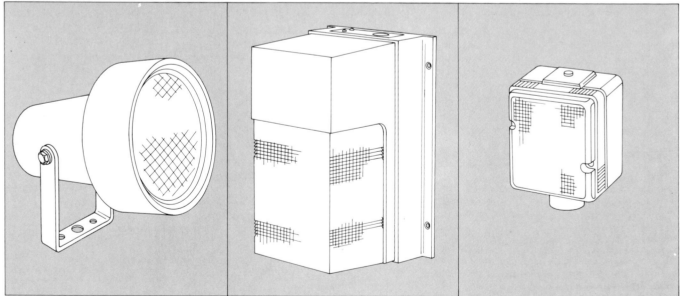

Three types of lighting fixture. The fixture on the left comes with a spot or flood lens and can be mounted either on the house or away from it. Fitted with a 50 watt high-pressure sodium lamp and a spot lens, it casts a cone of light with a base diameter roughly equal to the height of the fixture above the ground; fitted with the same type of lamp and a flood lens, it casts a cone of light with a base diameter roughly equal to one and a half times the height of the fixture above the ground. The fixture in the centre, which is for wall-mounting only, can also be fitted with a 50 watt high-pressure sodium lamp; if you position it 5 metres above the ground, it will light up an area of 5 metres on either side and at the front. Also designed for mounting on a wall, the photocell shown on the right can be used to control either a single lamp or a complete security lighting system up to the maximum wattage of 1,000 watts, automatically switching itself on at dusk and off again at dawn.

Mounting an Outside Wall Light

1 Fixing the backplate and the conduit. Mark the proposed location of the light—in this example, 1 metre or so below the soffit. Remove the lens from the unit, unscrew the lamp's mounting plate and take out the reflector. Hold the backplate against the wall and mark the position of the fixing screws. Using a masonry bit of the correct size, drill holes for the fixing screws and insert wall plugs. Secure the backplate to the wall.

Outside the loft, drill a 20 mm entry hole through the soffit, lining it up with the entry hole in the top of the light. Then cut a section of 20 mm plastic conduit long enough to reach from one hole to the other, with at least 50 mm to spare; this will protect the supply cable. Run the conduit between the two holes, allowing the overrun to project into the roof space. Use clip-type conduit saddles to secure the conduit to the wall, and a conduit adaptor to connect it to the light.

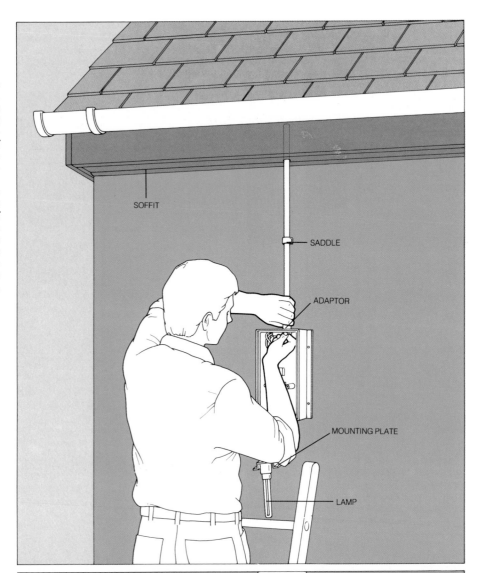

SOFFIT

SADDLE

ADAPTOR

MOUNTING PLATE

LAMP

2 Installing the supply cable. Inside the loft, mark where you want to connect into the lighting circuit cable—this is the mains cable which runs between lighting points and is usually fixed alongside one or more joists. Cut a length of 1 mm^2 two-core and earth cable long enough to reach from where you have just marked to the light, with some to spare. Ask a helper to push one end of the cable up through the conduit, then use cable clips to secure the section that runs into the loft, making sure that it is fixed at least 50 mm above the base of the joist.

At the lamp end, trim back about 75 mm of the cable sheathing. Then strip about 15 mm off the insulation of the live and neutral conductors. The earth wire will be bare, so you need to fit it with a length of green and yellow PVC sleeving, leaving the last 15 mm uncovered. Connect each wire to its appropriate terminal, pairing the live cable wire (red) with the live flex wire (brown), the neutral cable wire (black) with the neutral flex wire (blue), and the earth cable wire (green and yellow) with the earth flex wire (also green and yellow). Reassemble the lamp.

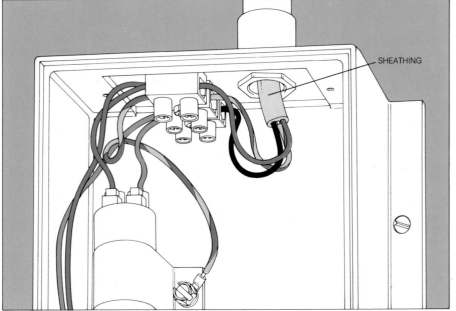

SHEATHING

3 **Installing the manual switch.** Mark where you want the switch; this can be placed at any convenient point inside the house, provided that the switch cable will run vertically to the joint box in the loft. Fix the mounting box in position. Run a length of 1 mm² two-core and earth cable between here and the intended point of connection to the mains cable, chasing the cable into the wall where necessary *(pages 66–71)*. Use cable clips to secure the section that runs into the loft. At the switch end, trim back the insulation of the live and neutral conductors and sleeve the earth wire.

Connect the earth wire to the terminal inside the mounting box, and the red and black wires to the terminals on the back of the switchplate. It makes no difference which way round you connect these two. Make sure, however, that you tag the black wire with red tape as a reminder that it is live whenever the switch is on. Screw the switchplate back into position.

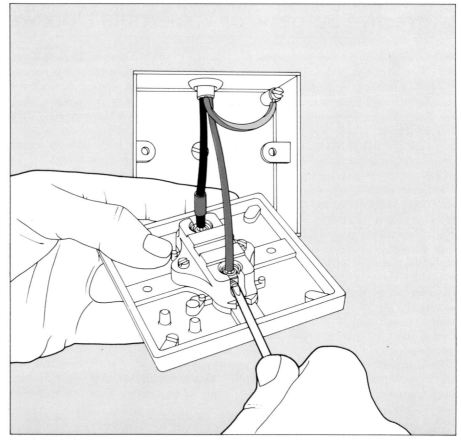

4 **Connecting the joint box.** With the power turned off at the consumer unit and the circuit fuse removed, cut the mains cable where you have marked it, stripping back the insulation of the live and neutral conductors and sleeving the bare earth wires *(opposite page, Step 2)*. Trim back the insulation of the new cables and conductors in the same way. Remove the cover of a four-terminal joint box and screw the base to the joist. Although the terminals are interchangeable, you must make sure that all the wires are joined up in the correct sequence.

Begin with the two stripped ends of the mains cable, connecting the red (live) wires to one terminal, the black (neutral) wires to a second terminal and the green and yellow (earth) wires to a third terminal. Next, link in the light cable, joining the black wire to the second terminal, the green and yellow wire to the third terminal and the red wire to the fourth terminal. Finally, connect up the switch cable, joining the red wire to the first terminal, the green and yellow wire to the third terminal and the black wire to the fourth terminal. Tag the black wire with red tape as a reminder that it is live whenever the switch is on. Fit the cover of the joint box back on, replace the fuse and restore the power.

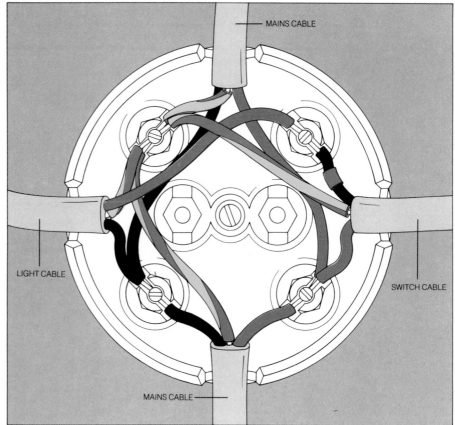

MAINS CABLE

LIGHT CABLE

SWITCH CABLE

MAINS CABLE

Corrective Surgery for Vulnerable Doorways

Most exterior doors are strong enough to be made virtually impregnable. There are exceptions to this rule. A hollow-core door—occasionally used because it is cheap—is too flimsy to provide even a modicum of security against attack. And good quality locks are a waste of money if doors and frames are in poor condition—rotten, badly secured, or with weak hinges.

Exterior wooden doors should have a solid core made of either hardwood or blockboard, and for greatest security they should be windowless. Letter boxes, which may otherwise allow access to the latch, should be placed as far from the latch as possible. If this is not practical, fit a metal letter-box shield that is open only at the bottom. To see who is outside, install a viewer *(below)*; models with a 180-degree field of vision make it impossible for anyone to duck out of sight.

Even the sturdiest doors are easy to break open if there is a weakness in the fittings, such as hinges, locks and security

chains. Exterior doors should have three good-quality hinges, and in each hinge two of the screws should penetrate through the frame into the masonry *(opposite page, left)*. A door chain, which can easily give way under impact and can also be sawn through, should be replaced with a door limiter *(opposite page, right, above)*.

A strike plate for a deadlocking bolt that consists of a simple metal sheet with a hole in it cannot protect the bolt from being forced with a crowbar, and should be replaced with a box-type strike plate *(page 32)*. Additional protection for the strike plate of a mortise lock or the strike box of a rim lock may be provided by a reinforcing bar—a strip of metal attached to the inside of the frame that distributes any impact from outside along the full length of the jamb *(page 20, above)*. To protect a door edge weakened by a mortise lock, fit security plates *(opposite page, right, below)*.

Timber frames that have been nailed instead of screwed in place can be prised

away from the wall. You can secure such frames with long, expanding masonry bolts *(page 20, below)*. If the doorstop in an external doorframe consists of separate strips of wood which are nailed or screwed to the jambs, expanding masonry bolts should be used to properly secure both the doorstop and the frame.

Finally, doors that themselves lack the strength to provide adequate security—for example, hollow-core doors that open from a flat on to a passageway—must be reinforced. For flush doors without glass or raised mouldings, use 16-gauge metal sheeting, which is thick enough to offer good security, but not too heavy for standard hinges. Allow a 6 mm clearance between the metal and the doorframe, and ask your sheet-metal supplier to drill holes for the bolts and to cut an opening for the letter box if you have one. The holes should be spaced at intervals of 300 mm and positioned 25 mm in from the edge of the metal sheeting *(page 21)*.

Installing a wide-angle viewer. At the centre of the door, at a height convenient for all members of the family, drill a hole as wide as the viewer shank from either side of the door, then insert the two halves of the viewer and screw them together. Screw the sections thumb-tight if the interior section is knurled; if it is slotted, use a coin to make the viewer snug.

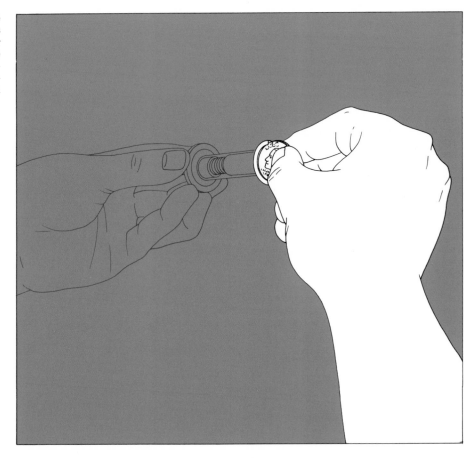

A door limiter. This device, designed to foil a forced entry by the "foot-in-the-door" method, provides greater security than most door chains but is only for use on wooden, inward-opening doors. To fit the limiter, first recess and secure the guide on the closing edge of the door 900 to 1200 mm from the bottom. Before securing the staple to the door jamb, check the action of the limiter: when the door is closed, the guide pegs should sit in the channels of the staple, and as it opens they should slide along smoothly until the door will open no further. To open the door wide, it must first be closed and the staple swung free of the guide pegs.

Deep fixings for a hinge. Two 70 mm hardened self-tapping masonry screws driven through the frame and 40 mm into the wall ensure that neither the hinge nor the frame can easily be jemmied. The masonry screws are alternated with two shorter wood screws—if inserted close together, the long screws could cause the masonry or brickwork to crumble. To drill the screw holes, use a wood bit until you reach the masonry, then change to a masonry bit.

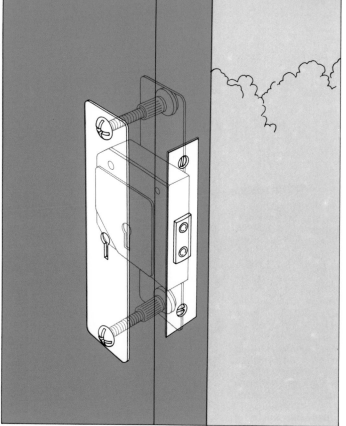

Security plates. To strengthen a door stile that has been weakened by the installation of a mortise lock, fit security plates on both sides of the door over the mortise area. Mark and drill holes above and below the lock body, then secure the plates with sleeve bolts—bolts in two sections that are screwed together from the inside of the door, leaving only a smooth convex button on the outside with nothing protruding to offer a purchase for crowbars or screwdrivers.

A reinforcement bar. In the case of an attempted forced entry, a metal strip screwed along the entire length of the doorjamb will protect the strike plate of a mortise lock, or the strike box of a rim lock, from being forced out or off. For the door on the right, which is fitted with both a rim lock and a mortise lock, a section of the metal strip is shaped to fit over the surface-mounted strike box. The size of the box and its position on the frame must be specified when ordering the reinforcement bar from your locksmith.

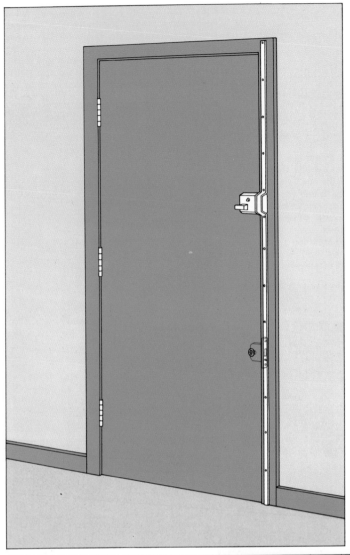

An expanding masonry bolt. Poorly fixed frames can be secured with expanding masonry bolts that penetrate through the jamb and at least two-thirds into the masonry or brickwork. Using bits the size of the bolt, drill through the jamb with a wood bit, then mark the length of the bolt on a masonry bit with masking tape and drill into the brickwork to that depth. Make a recess for the bolt head using a countersinking bit. Tighten the bolt slightly so that the captive nut is held loosely in the sleeve. Knock in the bolt. Using a cross-head screwdriver, tighten the screw, drawing the bolt into the sleeve and expanding the end to jam the whole bolt in place *(right)*. For a frame consisting of a single piece of wood, use four equally spaced bolts on each side. For a frame made in two strips—frame and doorstop—use eight bolts per side, set in pairs, four through the frame and four through both frame and doorstop.

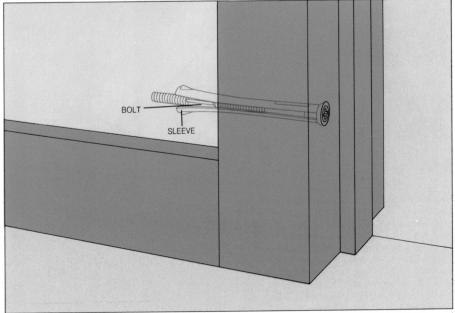

BOLT

SLEEVE

Metal Cladding for Wooden Doors

1 Preparing the door. Strip all the fittings off the door, remove the door from its hinges and lay it on the floor with the outside face upwards and the top end raised on a batten of wood. Place the metal sheet in position over the door, and mark fixing points through the pre-drilled holes in the sheet on to the door *(right)*. Remove the sheet and drill the bolt holes until the bit just penetrates the inside face of the door. Turn the door over and finish drilling the holes from the other side. Smooth away any burrs from the holes, using abrasive paper or a chisel, so that the sheet will lie flat against the door.

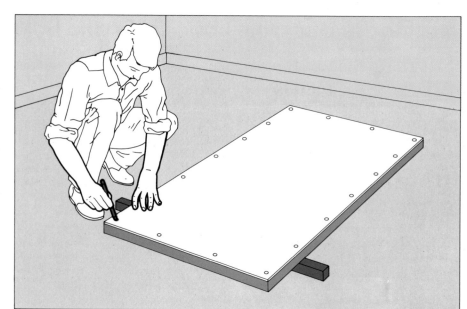

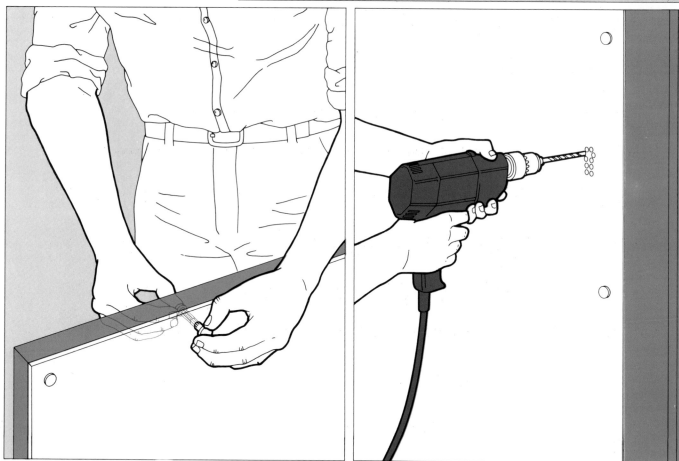

2 Fitting the metal cladding. With a helper holding the door upright, secure the metal sheet to the door with sleeve bolts *(page 19, right, below)*. Insert the shank of each bolt (with the convex button) from the outside of the door, then insert the corresponding screw from the inside and tighten with a screwdriver.

3 Drilling a hole for a key or cylinder. Rehang the door in the frame. Working from the reinforced side of the door and using the original hole as a guide, drill a series of small holes with a high-speed steel bit round the outline of the keyhole or cylinder hole. Knock through the perforations, then file the metal edges smooth. Refit the lock, letter box and any other door furniture.

Barring the Door: the Basic Locks and Bolts

Modern door locks operate on a simple and ancient principle. A rigid locking arm, called a bolt, is mounted in or on the door so that it can be slid into a socket, or strike plate, attached to the doorframe. The bolt is shot forwards and withdrawn by turning a key, which operates an intricate mechanism housed inside the lock body *(box, below)*. In addition to the bolt, most locks for back or side doors have a spring-operated latch which allows the door to be opened and closed with a handle or knob.

Many locks do not have the strength or complexity to provide much security. The springlatch, or nightlatch, *(opposite page, top)*, can be forced from outside with a knife inserted between door and jamb; a lever-operated lock with only two levers can also be forced or picked easily. These locks should only be used on internal doors.

Where security is important, always install a deadlock—a lock whose bolt can only be drawn back with a key. On some models, the deadlock can be overridden with a thumb turn; this is especially important in multi-occupancy buildings, or with children or old people in the house. Also, the lock should have at least a thousand "differs", or variations, so that it can be operated by only one key in every thousand made for the same lock design. Some models offer as many as 50,000 differs.

The main exit door of a house or flat should be fitted with both a mortise deadlock set in the closing edge of the door *(opposite, below, left)* and a rim lock mounted on the inside face; fit the mortise lock one-third of the door height from the bottom, and the rim lock an equivalent distance from the top. Side and back exit doors should have a sash lock—a mortise lock with both bolt and handle-operated latch *(opposite, below, right)*—and two security bolts mortised into the edge of the door about 150 mm from the top and bottom *(page 24, below, left)*. To take a good-quality mortise lock, the door stile should be at least 45 mm thick and 63 mm wide. Doors with thin stiles must be strengthened with security plates to take a mortise lock, or fitted with a high-quality dead-locking rim lock *(opposite page, centre)*.

In addition to the standard locks mentioned above, there are specialized locks designed for specific purposes or types of door *(pages 24–25)*. For doors requiring extra security, fit a multipoint lock with several bolts that secure the door at three or fours points. Hinge bolts protect the hinge edge of a door; while recommended for all doors, they are particularly useful on outward-opening doors with exposed hinges. French windows should be fitted with security bolts, and sliding patio doors with pressbolts. For garage or shed doors, choose from a range of padlocks and hasps.

The Levers and Pins That Work a Lock

Modern locks are of two principal types: lever locks and cylinder locks.

The plate-like levers of a lever lock *(right)* each have a slot divided by two flanges, and are held down by springs. When the lock's flat-bitted key is turned, its wards raise the levers to create a pathway along which the bolt knob can slide; at the same time, the key, or in some cases a key plate, engages the bolt and pushes it forwards. As the bolt engages fully and the key completes its turn, the levers fall again over the knob, deadlocking the bolt.

A cylinder lock contains sets of pins and springs in two cylinders—a smaller cylinder, called the plug, that fits within a larger cylinder, the housing. Both have rows of holes—at least five in the best locks—that line up when the bolt or latch is locked *(far right, above)*. In each hole of the housing, a spring presses against two pins—one from the housing, one in the plug—so that the top pin enters the corresponding hole in the plug, engaging the plug to keep it from turning.

A notched key lifts both of the pins in each hole *(bottom right)* so that the separation between the top pins and the plug pins coincides with the narrow space—called the shear line—between the plug and the housing. With the solid pins which engage the two cylinders pushed out of the way, the key can rotate the plug and move the cylinder rod, activating the latch or bolt.

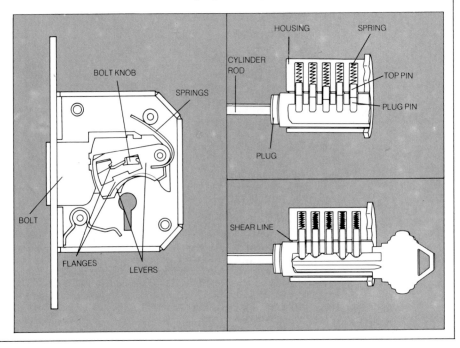

Guardians for Outside Doors

A springlatch rim lock. The case of this lock, mounted on the inside of the door, aligns with a strike box attached to the doorframe. The lock is operated by a key from outside and a thumb turn inside, and the latch can be held back in the case or locked in the strike box by a button on the case. Because the bevelled latch can easily be forced from outside, this common lock does not by itself provide good security.

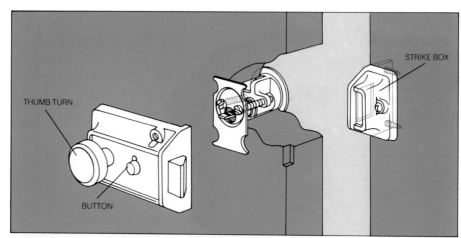

A deadlatch rim lock. A more sophisticated version of the springlatch (*above*), the bolt of this lock is automatically deadlocked by the auxiliary, triangular latch when the door is closed. The thumb turn inside can be deadlocked with a key, and the latch can be held back in the lock case by sliding the button. The casing is attached to the lugs on the mounting plate with screws that can be removed only when the door is open.

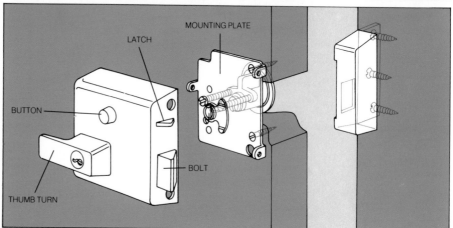

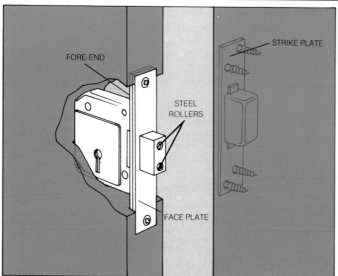

A five-lever mortise deadlock. The lock body fits into a mortise cut into the door; the fore-end and face plate are recessed in the door edge and secured with screws. The lock can be deadlocked with a key from both sides of the door, and the five levers ensure that the lock is hard to pick or force. The bolt is protected by a box-type strike plate in the doorjamb, and incorporates two steel rollers that rotate freely to frustrate attempts to saw through the bolt.

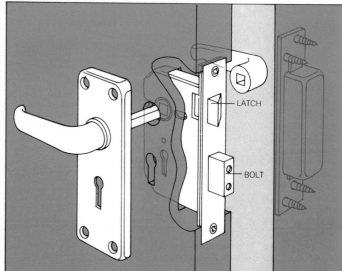

A sash lock. A mortise deadlock with a spring-operated latch combines a high degree of security with a convenient means of opening and closing the door. The bolt locking mechanism has the same built-in security features as the lock shown on the left. The latch is operated by a handle or knob on both sides of the door connected by a spindle, and is protected by handle plates.

Multipoint locks. Locks that secure several points around a door, with bolts thrown by a single key, may be either mortised into the door's leading edge *(right)* or surface-mounted *(far right)*. The latter type can be screwed directly to the door face with wood screws, but fitting a mortised multi-point requires special tools and careful carpentry *(pages 32–34)*. Because of their weight, multi-points are suitable only for sturdy doors.

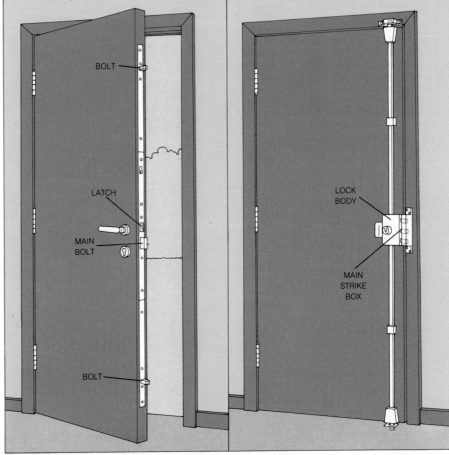

A security bolt. This simple bolt, mortised into the door's edge and operated from the inside with either a fluted key as shown here, or an ordinary flat key, can be used in addition to a main lock for extra security. On solid external doors, to give greatest security, two bolts should be set into the door's leading edge about 150 mm from the top and bottom; on French windows, set the bolts into the top and bottom edges so that one shoots into the frame head and the other into the sill *(pages 35–36)*. The keys should be kept handy in case of fire. With all-glass doors, security is limited if the lock is operated with a fluted key because the same key fits any number of similar bolts: a burglar can smash the glass and unlock the bolts with such a key.

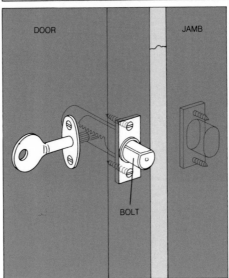

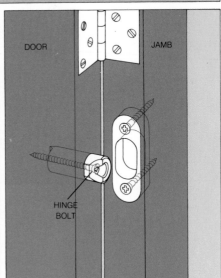

A hinge bolt. Particularly useful on doors that open outwards with exposed hinges, a hinge bolt provides simple, inexpensive and invisible security. The bolt is fixed into the door edge close to the hinge and a matching strike plate is recessed into the frame *(page 37)*. When the door is closed, the bolt enters the strike plate, ensuring that the door cannot be lifted out even if the hinges are sawn off or the pins removed.

Protection for Special Doors

Two ways to lock sliding doors. A pivoted metal bar drops from the doorframe to a socket on the edge of the sliding panel to lock this door securely in place *(below)*. A pin across the socket holds the bar in position and is pulled out to open the lock *(inset)*. When not needed, the bar swings up into a bracket on the doorframe.

For greater security, a keyed pressbolt at the top and base of the doors *(bottom)* locks the sliding and stationary panels together, so that the sliding panel cannot be slid open nor lifted out of its frame. Its screws are inside the casing, to prevent tampering.

Padlocks and hasps. A good padlock has a hardened steel shackle, a lock case of solid brass or laminated steel, and a five-pin cylinder *(page 22)*. The cylinder turns a rectangular drive bar to retract the bolts from notches in the shackle *(inset)*. The shackle then pops up, propelled by a spring near the lock base. In locking, a downward thrust on the shackle forces the bevelled bolts back until the shackle notches can engage them.

The ring of the hasp, called a staple, should be hardened steel. The hasp edges should be bevelled to ward off prising attacks.

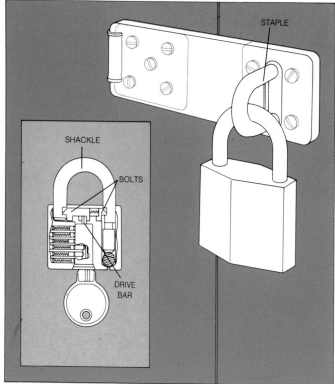

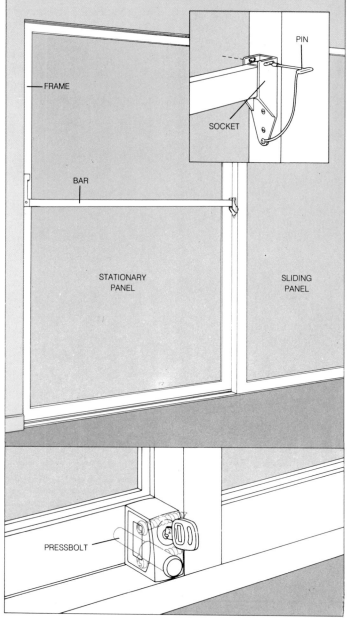

Putting On a Better Lock

Some improvements in the locks on your exterior doors can be very simple, involving nothing beyond a change of keys. Others require the replacement of existing locks or the addition of new locks. If you have a springlatch, for instance, it is advisable to add, or substitute, a more substantial lock with a deadlocking facility.

Before making large-scale alterations, ensure the maximum use of the good locks you already have. If the keys for a cylinder lock need changing, replace the cylinder *(below and opposite)*. In the case of a lever mechanism, it is possible to have the levers reset, but bear in mind that the cost of doing so can exceed the cost of a new lock.

The work involved in installing new locks depends on the lock. Rim locks—that is, locks mounted on the face of the door—are the simplest to install *(pages 28–29)*, but generally provide less security than a mortise lock housed in the door edge. When replacing an existing mortise lock, you may be able to buy one that fits the old mortise; for a new installation, however, you will have to cut a mortise in the door edge and drill holes for the cylinder or key and the latch spindle *(pages 30–31)*.

Careful marking and precise carpentry are essential for the cutting of mortises and recesses, which are also required for security and hinge bolts *(pages 35–37)*. No special tools are required, but when installing a multipoint lock a router will speed the cutting of the long recess for its mounting plate *(pages 32–34)*.

If you plan to use a lock with a bevelled latch, study the way your door swings, as the locksmith will need to know the "hand" of the door. If, like most exterior doors, your door opens inwards, stand outside the house and look at the hinges: a door with hinges on the right is a left-hand door; one with hinges on the left is a right-hand door. If your door opens outwards, tell the locksmith; such a door takes a lock that usually goes on a door of the opposite hand.

For mortised locks with bevelled latches, you must also bear in mind the width of the stop against which the door closes—if the spindle hole in the lock body is too close to the door edge, the handle or knob will strike against the stop and prevent the door from closing, or the stop may impede your hand when closed around the knob.

Make sure the lock you buy includes all the parts. Some rim locks have a paper template that can be folded to fit over the edges and face of the door, then pierced at specified points with a bradawl or nail to locate the holes for the lock. Check the screws that come with your lock; replace any that are too short for good security.

Replacing a Profile Cylinder

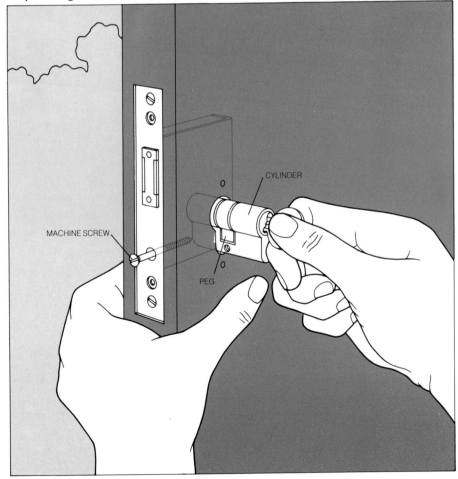

CYLINDER

MACHINE SCREW

PEG

Inserting the new cylinder. Remove the roses from around the keyhole. Unscrew the face plate, and then loosen the long machine screw that holds the cylinder in place. Insert the key and turn it so that the peg is aligned with the body of the cylinder. With your fingers and with the key still in the keyhole, push the cylinder towards you from the far side of the door so that the peg is clear of the hole and the cylinder protrudes far enough to offer a good grip. Then pull the cylinder out of the door. To insert the new cylinder, simply follow the instructions in reverse order.

Replacing a Round Cylinder

1 **Removing the old cylinder.** Unscrew the lock body from the face of the door to expose the mounting plate and the projecting cylinder rod *(below, left)*. Holding the cylinder rod end with one hand, unscrew the cylinder screws in the mounting plate to release the cylinder and rose, which can then be removed from the opposite side of the door *(below, right)*.

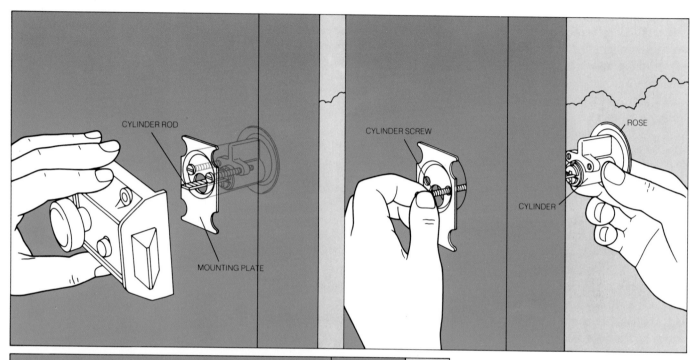

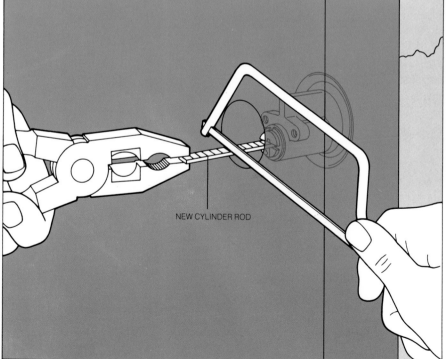

2 **Cutting the cylinder rod.** From the outside of the door, insert the new cylinder with its accompanying rose in the hole. Then, from inside the door, hold the projecting end of the cylinder rod with a pair of pliers; mark the rod with a hacksaw 4 mm beyond the face of the door *(left)*. Remove the cylinder and cut the rod off at the mark with the hacksaw. Replace the cylinder in the door, then reverse the procedures in Step 1 to secure the cylinder with the supplied screws through the mounting plate. Reattach the lock body.

Installing a Rim Lock

1 Marking the cylinder hole. Secure the door in an open position by knocking wedges under its bottom edge. On the inside of the door, fold the lock's template over the edge of the door along the line indicated, and tape it to the door. With a bradawl, pierce the point marked for the cylinder. If there is no template, measure from the edge of the lock to the centre of the cylinder hole, and transfer the measurement to the inside of the door.

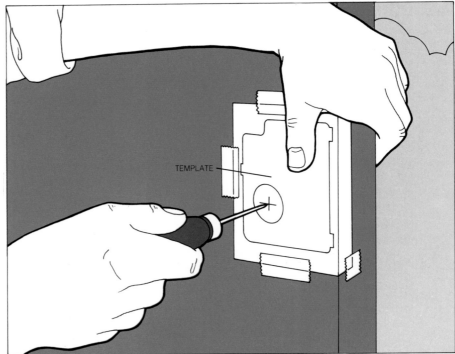

TEMPLATE

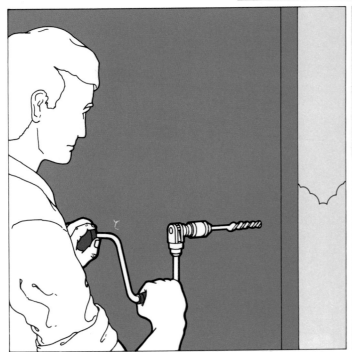

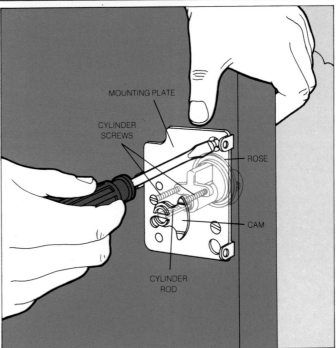

MOUNTING PLATE

CYLINDER SCREWS

ROSE

CAM

CYLINDER ROD

2 Drilling the holes. Drill a hole for the cylinder using a brace fitted with a 32 mm bit. Stop drilling when the point of the bit penetrates the far side; complete the hole by drilling inwards from the other side of the door.

3 Fixing the mounting plate. Insert the cylinder and rose into the hole from the outside of the door following the instructions on page 27, Steps 2 and 3. Position the mounting plate on the inside face of the door, slotting it over the end of the cylinder rod. Secure the first of the two cylinder screws linking the mounting plate to the cylinder. Turn the key in the lock to turn the cam, exposing the second cylinder screw hole, and fix the second screw. Screw the mounting plate to the door (*above*). Check that all the screws are tight, so that the cylinder is fixed firmly to the mounting plate and the mounting plate to the door.

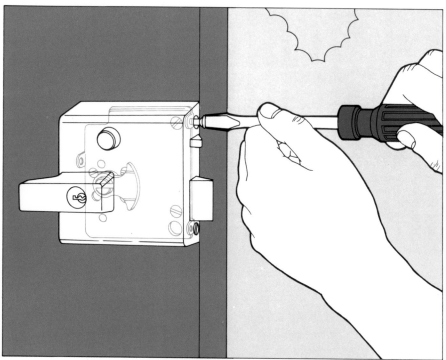

4 **Fitting the lock body.** Remove the key, returning the cam to its original position. Place the body of the lock over the mounting plate and check that the lock operates correctly. Secure the lock body to the lugs on the mounting plate using the screws provided *(left)*.

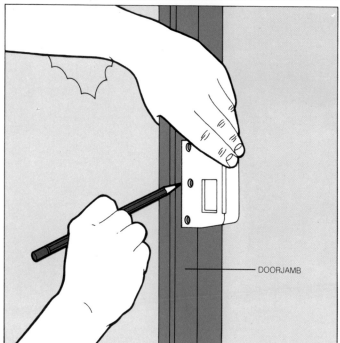

DOORJAMB

5 **Positioning the strike box.** Close the door and make marks on the doorjamb corresponding to the top and bottom of the lock body. Open the door and square round the doorjamb from the marks. Align the strike box with the marked lines on the jamb and pencil round the perimeter of its mounting plate *(above)*.

6 **Chiselling the recess.** Using a mallet and a wood chisel, cut along the outline you have just marked. Then chisel away the wood from within the outline to the depth of the strike box mounting plate *(above)*. Check the fit as you work to ensure that the plate fits snugly into the frame. Secure the strike box with the screws provided *(inset)*. When the door is closed, the deadlatch of the lock will slot into the strike plate hole.

Installing a Sash Lock

1 **Drilling the mortise.** Hold the lock body against the closing edge of the door and mark along its top and bottom edges. Between the two horizontal lines, mark a vertical line centred on the door edge. Choose a spade drill bit the width of the lock body, and mark the depth of the lock body on its shaft with a piece of tape. Holding the drill firmly to prevent the bit from wandering, drill a series of holes along the vertical line to the depth of the tape *(right)*.

If you are nervous about keeping the drill straight and at right angles as you bore into the door edge, use a drill guide. A lock collar on one of the rods can be set to stop the drill when the bit has reached the depth of the mortise.

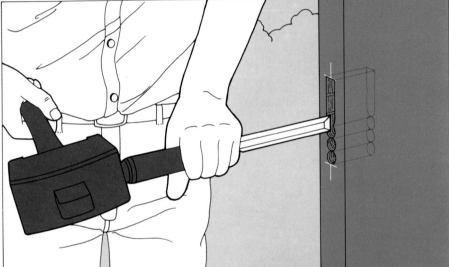

TAPE

CENTRE LINE

2 **Squaring the mortise.** Between the horizontal lines on the door edge, mark two vertical lines to join up the edges of the drilled holes. Use a mallet and a chisel with its bevel facing inwards to chip out the remaining wood and square the mortise *(right)*. When most of the wood has been removed, shave the sides of the mortise flat with the chisel blade without using the mallet.

3 **Cutting the recess.** Fit the lock body into the mortise and mark round the fore-end with a pencil. Remove the lock body. Using a bevelled chisel, cut round the marked outline to the depth of the fore-end. With the bevel of the chisel towards the door edge, chip out the recess to the same depth *(right)*. If your lock has a secondary face plate to be secured over the fore-end attached to the lock body, remember to allow for both thicknesses. Check the depth of the recess as you work by holding the lock body while you test-fit the fore-end and, where necessary, the face plate.

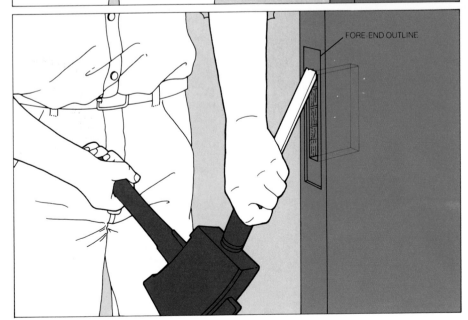

FORE-END OUTLINE

4 **Marking the cylinder hole.** Against one side of the door, align the lock body with the mortise, holding the fore-end and, if there is one, the face plate, flush with the door edge. Insert a pencil through the cylinder hole and mark its outline on the door *(right)*. If your lock works with levers and does not have a cylinder hole, mark through the keyhole with a bradawl. Mark the position for the spindle that connects the handles through the upper hole in the lock body, then mark up the other side of the door in the same way.

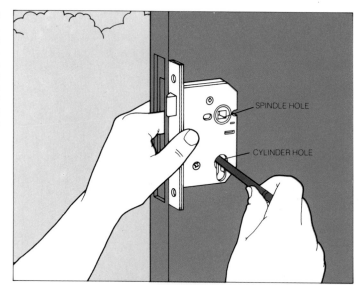

SPINDLE HOLE

CYLINDER HOLE

5 **Drilling the cylinder hole.** Using an 18 mm and a 12 mm spade bit to match the standard size of the cylinder profile, drill two holes one above the other within the cylinder outline through one side of the door into the mortise *(right)*. Then drill the holes from the other side of the door. Chisel between the two drilled holes to make a single hole matching the cylinder profile. Using a bit with a diameter slightly larger than the cross-section of the spindle, drill on the upper mark through one side of the door into the mortise. Then drill the hole from the other side of the door.

6 **Fitting the lock body and handles.** Insert the lock body in the mortise. Insert the cylinder into its hole, test the lock with the key, then secure the cylinder with the machine screw *(page 26)*. Secure the lock body in the mortise by driving the screws provided through its fore-end *(right)*, then attach the face plate over the fore-end. Slot the spindle through the upper hole in the lock body and attach the handle plates and handles with the screws provided *(inset)*.

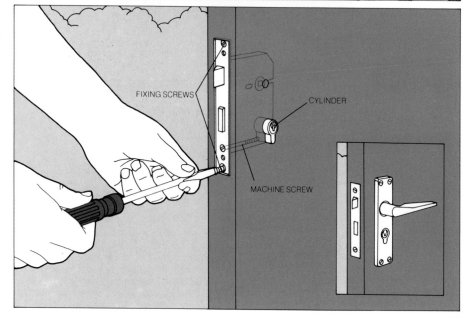

FIXING SCREWS

CYLINDER

MACHINE SCREW

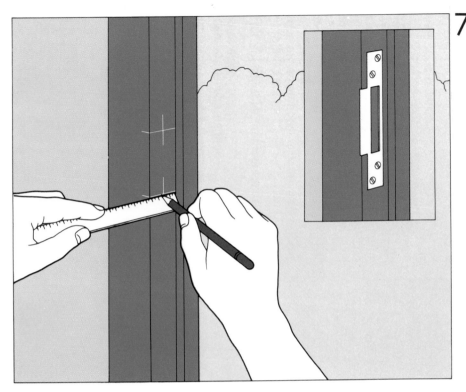

7 Securing the strike box. Throw the bolt of the lock by turning the key, then close the door against the jamb and mark the jamb along the top of the latch and the bottom of the bolt. Square these lines round the inside face of the jamb. On the door, measure between the door edge and the centre of the bolt, then transfer this measurement to the inside face of the jamb *(left)* and draw a vertical line between the two horizontal lines. Following the same procedures as for the lock mortise, drill and chisel out a mortise in the jamb for the strike box. Insert the strike box in the mortise, pencil round the face plate, then remove the strike box and chisel out a recess for the face plate. Secure the strike box in the jamb with the fixing screws provided *(inset)*.

Installing a Mortised Multipoint Lock

1 Marking up the door. Take the door off its hinges and set it in a clamp, with the closing edge facing upwards; use pieces of 50 by 25 mm timber either side of the door to increase stability. Mark the door edge 150 mm from the top and bottom, then trim the lock's mounting plate with a hacksaw to fit between the two marks. Lay the assembled lock face downwards between the top and bottom marks on the closing edge of the door, and draw along both sides of the mounting plate to mark the lock's final position in the centre of the door's closing edge.

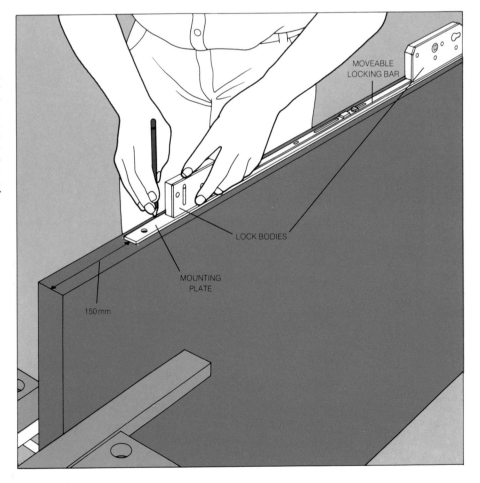

MOVEABLE LOCKING BAR

LOCK BODIES

MOUNTING PLATE

150 mm

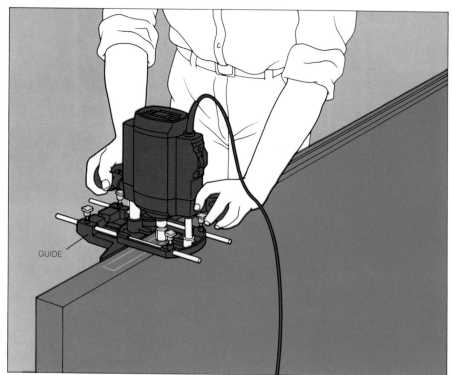

2 Cutting the first recess. Fit a router with a cutting bit that matches the width of the mounting plate, then set the blade to the depth of the mounting plate and adjust its guide to centre the bit on the door edge. Working carefully along the door edge, cut out a recess within the marked outline. Square off the corners at the ends of the recess with a wood chisel.

GUIDE

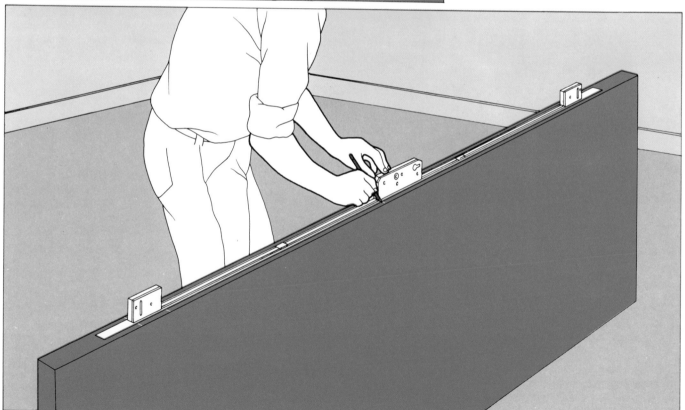

3 Marking up for the mortises. Lay the lock face downwards in the newly cut recess. Ensure that the mounting plate fits snugly and that it lies flush with the door edge; if it does not lie flush, chisel away more wood to deepen the recess. Mark the positions of the locks on the door edge *(above)*. Mark the centre point and depth of each lock and then cut a mortise for each using the technique shown on pages 30–31. Check that all the lock bodies slot easily into the mortises.

4 **Making room for the locking bar.** Fit the router with a bit which is 3 mm wider than the lock's moveable locking bar behind the mounting plate, and adjust the depth gauge of the router to the thickness of the moveable locking bar plus a couple of millimetres. Adjust the guide to centre the bit, then cut the second recess for the locking bar along the centre of the first recess for the mounting plate, between the top and bottom mortises only *(below)*.

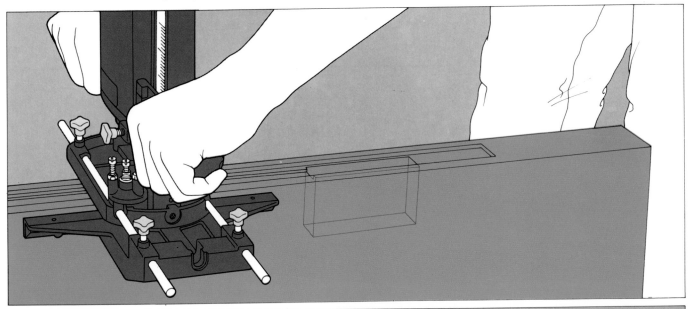

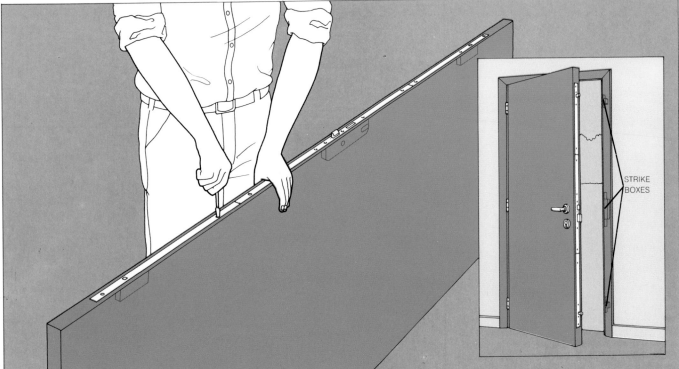

STRIKE BOXES

5 **Securing the lock.** Following the instructions on page 31, drill holes for the lock cylinder and the handle spindle through the centre mortise. Lay the assembled lock in position in the door, slotting each lock body into its separate mortise. Secure the cylinder with its machine screw *(page 26)*, then test the lock with its key. Secure the mounting plate in its recess with the screws provided *(above)*, and attach the handles and handle plates. Rehang the door, replacing the old hinges with more substantial ones if necessary to bear the increased weight of the door. Fit strike boxes in the doorjamb for each of the locks as you would for an ordinary mortise lock, as shown on page 32, Step 7.

A Security Bolt for French Windows

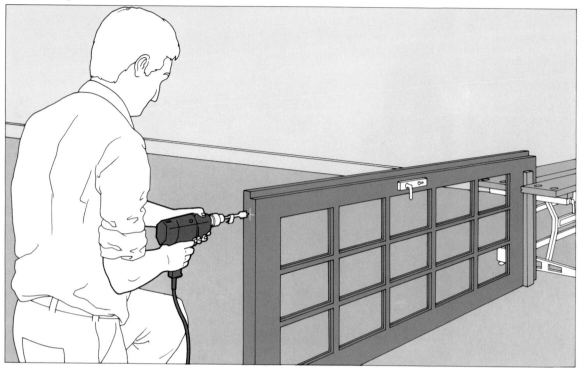

1 **Drilling the bolt hole.** Take the door off its hinges and secure it in a clamp with its closing edge upwards; use two pieces of 50 by 25 mm timber placed vertically either side of the door to increase stability. Mark across the top edge of the door about 50 mm from the closing edge. Choose a bit the same diameter as the bolt and mark the length of the bolt on the bit with a piece of tape. In the centre of the line across the top edge of the door, drill a hole for the bolt.

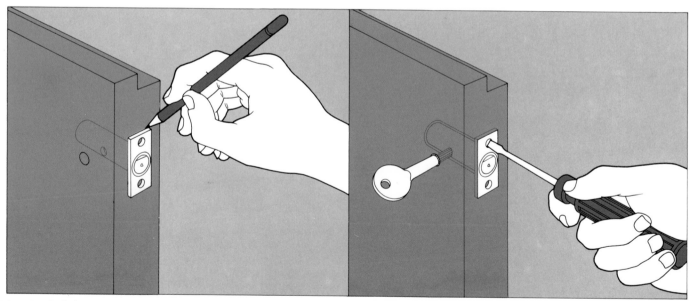

2 **Inserting the bolt.** Square the line across the top edge of the door on to the interior face, and mark off the distance from the top of the wound-in bolt to the keyhole. With a 6 mm bit, drill at the marked point until the bit breaks through into the bolt hole. Insert the bolt and draw round the edge of the face plate *(above, left)*. Remove the bolt and chip away a recess for the face plate *(page 30, Step 3)*. Reinsert the bolt, insert the key, and test the bolt. Leaving the key in place, insert and tighten the face plate screws *(above, right)*. Finally, screw the rose over the keyhole.

3 **Making the strike plate hole.** Rehang the door. Wind out the bolt, and mark it with lipstick *(right)*. Wind in the bolt, close the door, then wind out the bolt again firmly to mark the position for the strike plate on the doorframe.

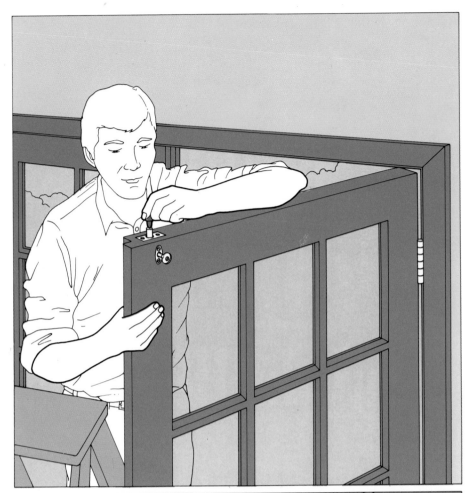

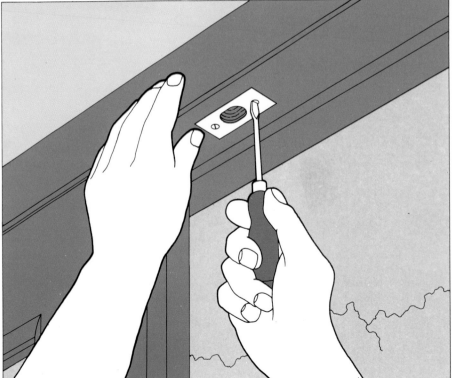

4 **Inserting the strike plate.** With the door open, wind out the bolt and measure its length. Drill a hole to this length at the marked spot on the frame. Position the strike plate over the hole; mark round the plate and chisel a recess for it. Check that the bolt slides smoothly into the hole. Secure the strike plate with the screws provided.

Installing a Hinge Bolt

1 **Marking the door.** Mark across the hinge edge of the door 75 mm below the top hinge, then mark the centre of the line. Snip the top off a panel pin, and knock the pin into the spot where the two lines meet. Close the door gently to make an indentation in the doorframe with the top of the pin, marking the position for the strike plate hole.

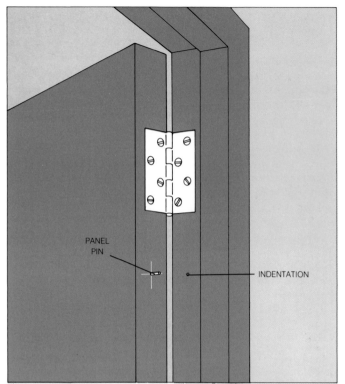

PANEL
PIN

INDENTATION

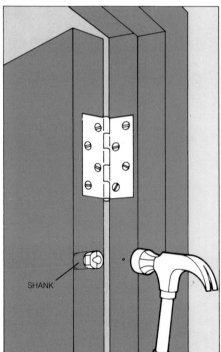

SHANK

2 **Inserting the bolt.** Pull out the panel pin. With tape, mark off the length of the bolt on a drill bit the same diameter as the bolt. Drill into the marked spot to the correct depth. Tap the bolt into the door *(above)*. If the bolt is bevelled, as in the example illustrated here, ensure that the bevel is the right way round: the slope should face you as you work.

3 **Installing the strike plate.** Place the strike plate on the frame so that the marked spot falls in the centre of the hole. Mark round the strike plate. Choose a bit the width of the strike plate hole, and mark the length of the exposed bolt on the bit with tape. Drill two holes, one immediately above and one below the marked spot to the depth indicated. Chisel away the excess wood within the outline *(above)*; then chisel a recess for the strike plate, and screw it in place *(inset)*.

Securing Windows Against Forced Entry

Even a novice burglar generally knows how to unlatch a sliding sash window with a knife blade inserted between the sashes. Unless a window is fitted with special break-resistant panes, it is relatively easy to cut or break away enough glass to reach inside and undo the latch. However, any of a number of locking devices can guard windows against all but a persistent intruder. Some of them are clearly visible additions, and are therefore useful as deterrents. The mere sight of a formidable-looking lock can discourage a would-be burglar from attempting entry.

Ideally, every window easily accessible from outside should be fitted with a lock, but any window that might become an emergency exit in a fire should be locked in such a way that it can be opened quickly and easily from inside. Locks that work

with a key should be keyed alike, so that one key opens any window; a key should be kept where it is handy for use from inside but cannot be reached from outside.

There are many ways of securing sash windows, horizontal sliding windows and casement windows. Any lock with exposed screw heads, however, can be simply unscrewed by an intruder once the window is broken, so when installing these types of lock you should deface the heads of the screws that come with the locks, or use non-retractable "prison" screws *(below)*.

For sliding sash windows, one of the simplest security devices is the sash stop, which can be positioned to allow the sash to open fractionally for ventilation *(opposite page, above, left)*. Mounted near the side of the window, the stop prevents the sashes from being jemmied open. A less obtrusive

lock for sash windows is the dual screw—a barrel which is set into the inside sash frame, and which contains a bolt that is screwed into the outer frame *(opposite page, above, centre)*.

Casement windows open outwards and are therefore more difficult to make secure. They may be fitted with a number of devices which employ bolts or hinged brackets *(opposite page, above, right, and below)*. Alternatively, you can install security bolts of the type illustrated on page 24. For additional protection you can replace the old fastener with a locking handle, but these should not be used on their own; if the handle is broken off, the window can be opened with ease.

Horizontally sliding windows are best secured by the methods that are used for sliding doors *(page 25)*.

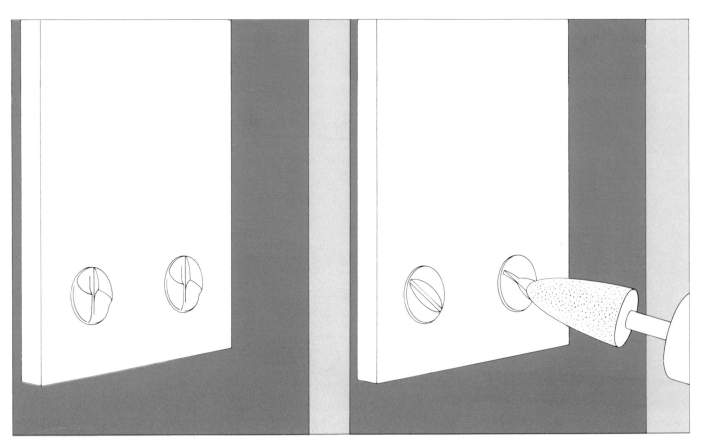

Putting in screws for keeps. A non-retractable screw *(above, left)* has a special head, making the screw impossible to remove without destroying screw or framing. Before tightening such screws, be certain that the lock you are fastening is positioned correctly. If non-retractable screws are not readily available, use the tip of a conical grindstone in an electric drill to erase the screw slot *(above, right)*. Grind only along the sides of the slot; excessive grinding can weaken the screw.

Locks for Windows

A sash stop. When the bolt of this simple sash stop is wound out with a flanged key, it prevents the sashes sliding past each other but allows a small gap top or bottom for ventilation. To install the lock, cut a recess for the face plate and drill a hole for the barrel in the side of the top sash no more than 100 mm above the top rail of the bottom sash; secure the face plate with the screws provided. Screw the strike plate—which protects the wood when the bolt is wound out and the window is open—to the top rail of the lower sash. For wide windows, fit a sash stop on each side.

Dual screws. In this simple sash-window lock, a threaded barrel screwed into the inner sash houses a bolt that is turned with a flanged key to engage a strike plate set in the outer sash. To install the lock, drill a hole 10 mm wide through the inner sash, and drill a further 15 mm into the outer sash. Screw the barrel into the inner sash. Cut a recess for the strike plate in the outer sash and secure it over the hole with the screws provided. For large windows, fit two dual screws.

A bolt lock. The lever bolt on this lock for timber casement windows is swung into place with a knob which can be locked with a simple key. There are a number of key variations. To fit the lock, hold the lock body on the closed sash and drive the screws directly into the wood. The strike plate may be either recessed into the frame or surface mounted *(below)*; a slot is cut into the frame behind the strike plate for the bolt.

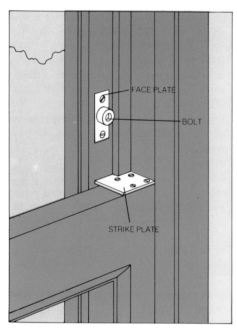

FACE PLATE

BOLT

STRIKE PLATE

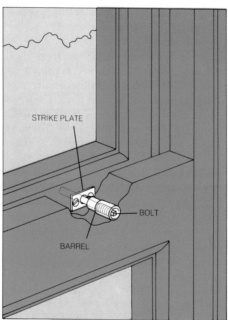

STRIKE PLATE

BOLT

BARREL

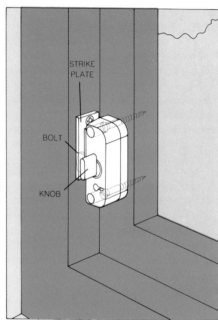

STRIKE PLATE

BOLT

KNOB

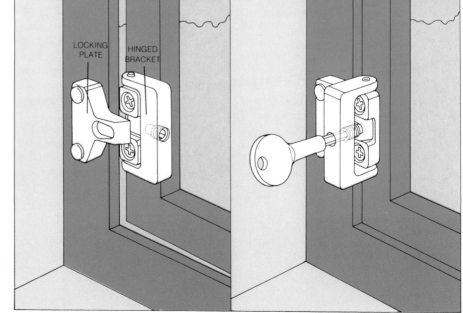

LOCKING PLATE

HINGED BRACKET

A hinged lock. This lock, for metal casement windows only, consists of two sections: a hinged bracket with an in-built screw lock and a locking plate *(right)*. To lock the window *(far right)*, the hinged bracket is folded over the lip of the locking plate, and is locked into place with a fluted key. To install, first mark the position for the hinged bracket on the opening frame. Drill holes for the screws, and attach the hinged bracket. Place the locking plate in position, mark and drill the screw holes and screw the locking plate on. A variation of this may be fitted to timber casement windows.

Safes and Vaults: Fortresses Within the House

For priceless objects and crucially important legal documents, the only adequate safeguard against burglary and fire is a rented safe-deposit box in a bank vault. But most safe-deposit boxes are too small for bulky valuables and too inconvenient for objects or papers you use frequently—silver cutlery, cameras, financial records and the like. The best way to protect such items is to store them in a home safe or burglar and fire-resistant strong room as shown on page 45.

Before choosing a safe, decide whether you are concerned more about burglary or about fire—protection from both is rarely combined in a single safe. Burglary safes have thick steel bodies, sophisticated combination locks and hardened-steel bolts, but papers inside may char in a fire. A fire safe, which is cheaper, lighter and more spacious, has a double shell of thin sheet metal filled with several centimetres of insulation. Some have reinforced doors and combination locks, but these features are only minor deterrents to a thief—a burglar can crack a fire safe in minutes by peeling away the sheet metal.

A fire safe does more than simply block the flow of heat. Its insulation—a crumbly, crystalline mixture of lightweight concrete and granules of vermiculite (a form of mica)—contains a large proportion of water. Usually, the water is locked into the crystal structure. But a fire disrupts the crystals, releasing the water and turning it into steam, in the process absorbing great amounts of heat. The steam, which filters through small vents outside the safe, may crumple and discolour papers, but they will stay legible and flexible enough to handle. Since the water of crystallization is so easily released by heat, old safes may have lost their fire protection; for this reason purchase of a used safe is not advised.

An ordinary fire-resistant cabinet (opposite page, above, left) will protect papers against fire, but a reinforced safe with a combination lock (opposite page, above, centre) will provide additional security. Also available are special low-temperature safes (opposite page, above, right) designed for floppy discs, tapes, photographic transparencies and other articles easily damaged by heat or condensation. Replace any safe that has been in a fire; its fire resistance is destroyed.

In contrast to a fire safe, which provides absolute protection for a specified period, a burglary safe is an uncertain safeguard, for no safe can resist sophisticated cutting tools. Most home burglary safes can withstand sledge hammers, drills and crowbars for only a few minutes. But a number of features will increase the security of your safe. It should have a combination lock; a relocking device, to fasten the bolts automatically if a burglar tries to drill through the lock or punch it out of its housing; a concealed hardened-steel plate to protect the lock and bolts; and dog-bolts or steel hooks to secure the hinge side of the door.

An important factor to consider when choosing your safe is insurance. The Association of Burglary Insurance Surveyors grade the value of the contents of safes, with a list of recommended safes for each grade. To satisfy your insurance company, you may have to have both the type of safe and its installation approved. For very valuable items it may be that the insurers will not sanction some D.I.Y. installations.

Insurance considerations apart, the style of safe you buy and the method of installation depend largely on the construction of your house and the amount of storage space you need. At the bottom of the scale are hideaway safes. Little more than strongboxes, they lack the strength and size of a normal safe but are unobtrusive and easy to install—some can be fitted by removing a single brick. If your house has a concrete floor free of damp and protected from flooding, you can dig a hole in the floor and pour new concrete round a small in-floor safe (opposite page, below, centre). If you have cavity walls, you can fit a wall safe (opposite page, below, left) in the same fashion, by removing a number of bricks and then mortaring round the safe. For larger objects—a collection of pictures or bulky photographic equipment, for instance—you may need a steel security cabinet (opposite page, below, right).

Most people choose a freestanding safe of moderate size. You must secure such a safe firmly, otherwise a burglar may cart it away. If the safe is to stand on a strong concrete floor, you can increase its weight and strength by getting the dealer to encase it in a solid concrete block, or by building a shell of concrete blocks around it (page 44). With less labour, you can install the safe in the traditional way, fastening it to a floor or into a false wall (pages 42–43). Use your ingenuity to find locations that will delay or baffle a burglar—for example, set the safe into the wall at the back of a wardrobe, alongside a heating duct, behind the contents of a bookcase or kitchen cabinet, or beneath a staircase.

If you have a centrally controlled alarm system (pages 62–63), you can protect the area round the safe with a motion detector, a pressure mat and a smoke detector to guard against cutting torches. Keep the sensors inconspicuous, so they do not betray the location of the safe; and keep the existence of the safe a secret—remarks by talkative children or neighbours often attract burglars.

The most difficult part of the installation job itself is handling the weight of the safe. With a crew of strong helpers, you can move a small safe with an ordinary sack barrow, as long as you do not need to use a stairway. If your new safe weighs more than 200 kilograms, ask the dealer to move it for you with hydraulic hand lifts. Many dealers will also arc-weld angle irons or mounting brackets to the safe according to your specifications.

Sure Protection for Valuables

A fire-resistant filing cabinet. Available in two, three and four-drawer sizes, a cabinet can hold objects or large amounts of paper. Inner and outer sheet-metal shells sandwich 38 mm layers of fire-resistant insulation; additional insulation in the front panel of each drawer and in the horizontal partitions between drawers makes each drawer an independent compartment.

A safe for papers. The safe has both the fire-resistant properties of an insulated cabinet and many of the features of a burglar-resistant safe, including a combination lock. Like all fire-resistant safes, it is freestanding only—drilling fixing holes through the sheet-metal casing would destroy the integrity of the insulation.

A safe for films and stamps. This expensive low-temperature safe protects objects easily damaged by heat and high humidity. The outer container is built like an ordinary fire safe but an airtight inner container of wood and insulating plastic provides extra protection for its contents.

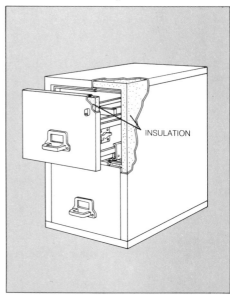

INSULATION

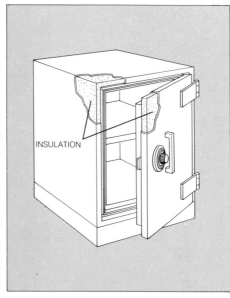

INSULATION

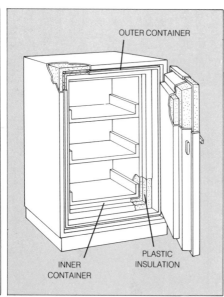

OUTER CONTAINER

INNER CONTAINER

PLASTIC INSULATION

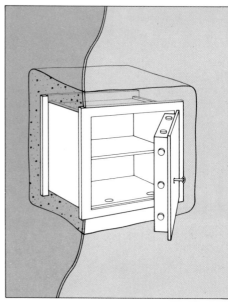

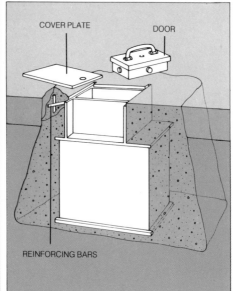

COVER PLATE

DOOR

REINFORCING BARS

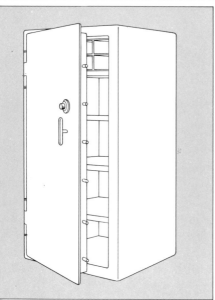

A burglar-resistant wall safe. This 39 kilogram safe is made of 6 mm steel, with seamless electric welds at all joints. Its door, a steel plate 12 mm thick, is fastened with a sophisticated three-tumbler combination lock and hardened-steel bolts; heavy steel hooks interlock with a flange on the body to prevent a burglar from cracking the safe by attacking the hinges.

A safe to bury in the floor. Inexpensive, easy to conceal, fire-resistant and extremely difficult to crack, this type offers advantages that may outweigh its difficulty of installation and relatively limited capacity. Almost all its strength is built into the 45 mm steel door, secured by four 25 mm bolts of hardened steel. The body is protected by a solid block of concrete which is reinforced with steel bars.

A cabinet for guns and furs. The security cabinet, meant for objects too large to fit inside an ordinary safe, comes in heights up to 1760 mm and widths up to 900 mm. The model sketched above is 1760 mm high, 630 mm wide and 210 kilograms in weight. Its body is 36 mm steel plate, and its 10 mm steel door is fastened by 12 steel bolts, six on each side.

Building a Safe Into a Timber-Frame Wall

1 **Building a false wall.** Cut away the wall covering round the planned location of the safe and, for a safe narrower than the space between studs there, nail horizontal 100 by 50 mm noggings between the studs of the existing wall, 12 mm above and below the safe location; add cleats under the lower nogging. Mark head and sole plates for the false wall with stud locations that match the locations of the existing studs. Nail the sole plate to the floor, spacing it out from the existing wall to accommodate the depth of the safe. Nail studs to the head plate, slide this assembly over the sole plate, nail the head plate to the ceiling joists and toenail the studs to the sole plate. Install noggings and cleats in the new wall to match those in the original wall.

For a safe wider than the stud spacing *(inset)*, cut away an existing stud 50 mm above and below the planned location of the new safe and build a frame as described above. Then nail the frame to the cut-off stud and add a vertical 100 by 50 to complete an opening the width of the safe.

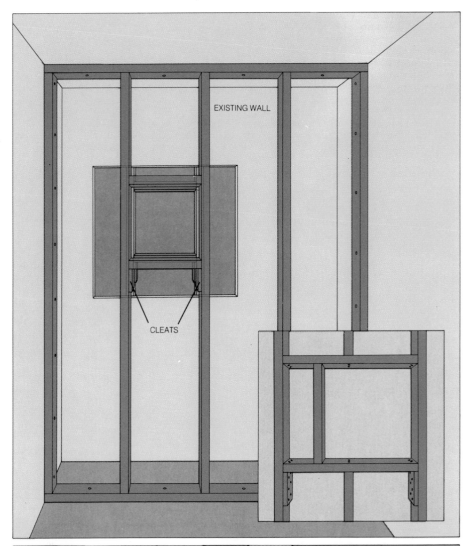

EXISTING WALL

CLEATS

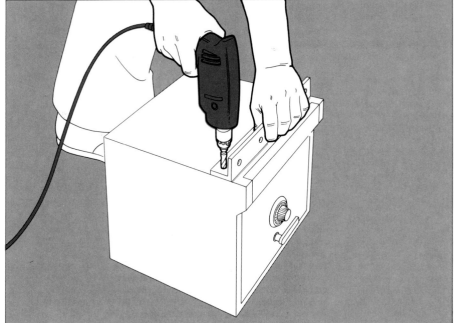

2 **Attaching the mounting brackets.** If your safe does not come with mounting flanges, attach a 40 by 6 mm steel angle iron to each side of the safe, 6 mm further from the front than the thickness of the plasterboard you will use. Drill 12 mm holes at 100 mm intervals along the centre of each flange of the angle iron and use it as a template to drill matching holes through the sides of the safe *(right)*. Fasten the angles to the safe with 12 mm coach bolts, round bolt heads facing out. Chisel a 6 mm recess for the angles at the front of the mounting studs to make a flat surface for the plasterboard.

3 **Installing the safe.** With the aid of a helper, slide the safe into the frame, shim the safe until it is level and fasten it to the studs with 12 mm coach bolts 50 mm long. Round the heads of the bolts with a grinder as shown on page 38. To complete the installation, attach plasterboard sheets to the new stud frame.

SHIMS

Bolting a Safe to the Floor

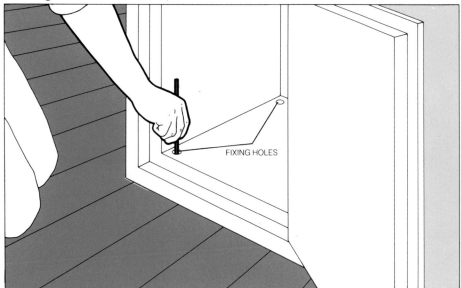

FIXING HOLES

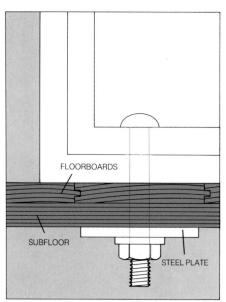

FLOORBOARDS

SUBFLOOR

STEEL PLATE

1 **Marking the holes.** If you want to bolt a safe to the floor, get the manufacturer to pre-drill the fixing holes when you order it. Position the safe where you want it, mark the corners of the safe on the floor, then mark where you are going to drill the holes in the floor *(above)*.

2 **Fastening the safe.** For a timber floor that is accessible from underneath, drill 12 mm holes at the marks for 75 mm long coach bolts and attach the nuts from beneath, using steel plates 75 mm square as washers. If you do not have access to the underside of the floor, use 12 mm anchor bolts to fasten the safe to the subfloor or joists.

For a concrete floor, use one of the masonry fasteners shown on page 55. Drill pilot holes at least 75 mm deep, using a carbide-tipped masonry bit and a hammer drill, then fasten the safe with rag bolts.

Encasing a Safe in Concrete Blocks

1 Building the base. At a corner of the basement floor lay a 19 mm mortar bed at least 800 mm wider and 200 mm longer than the safe; cover the bed with 150 by 150 mm wire mesh and add another 19 mm of mortar. Working from the corner, cover the mortar with a course of concrete blocks; use a hammer and cold chisel to cut channels for reinforcing bars in each block before it is set in position. Make the mortar joints between blocks and between the blocks and the wall 9 mm thick.

Lay pieces of 9 mm reinforcing bar in the channels of the blocks round all four edges *(inset)*. At the corners, use a pipe to bend the ends of the bars to a 90-degree angle, overlap the bent bars and fasten the overlapping ends with tie wire. Fill the blocks with mortar, trowelled off flush with the tops. At the location of the safe, make a platform of broken block cemented with mortar.

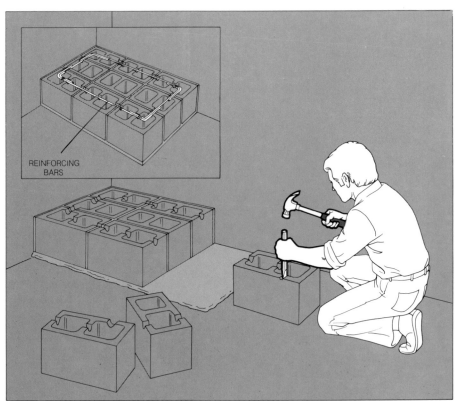

REINFORCING BARS

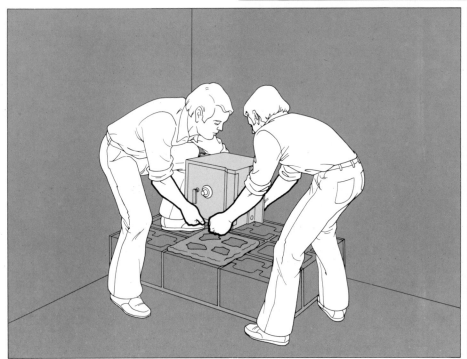

2 Installing the safe. Bolt 75 by 6 mm vertical angle irons to the sides of the safe *(page 42)*, 185 mm in from the front, or ask the safe dealer to weld them on. With a helper, set the safe on the mortar bed. Lay courses of blocks behind the safe and along the short edges of the enclosure, with 9 mm mortar joints between the courses; fill the gaps between the blocks and the safe with mortar, concrete bricks or concrete half blocks, depending on the size of the gaps. On top of the safe lay a mortar bed or a course of concrete bricks, level with the concrete blocks on each side, then lay a final course of blocks matching the bottom course *(Step 1)*, but do not fill the blocks with mortar in this step of the job.

3 Reinforcing the blocks. Make a 90-degree bend at one end of several reinforcing bars and push the bars down through the cores of the outside blocks as far as possible. Lay horizontal reinforcing bars in the channels round the edges of the top course of blocks *(Step 1)*. Fill the cores of all the blocks with mortar, then cover the cores with a course of concrete bricks.

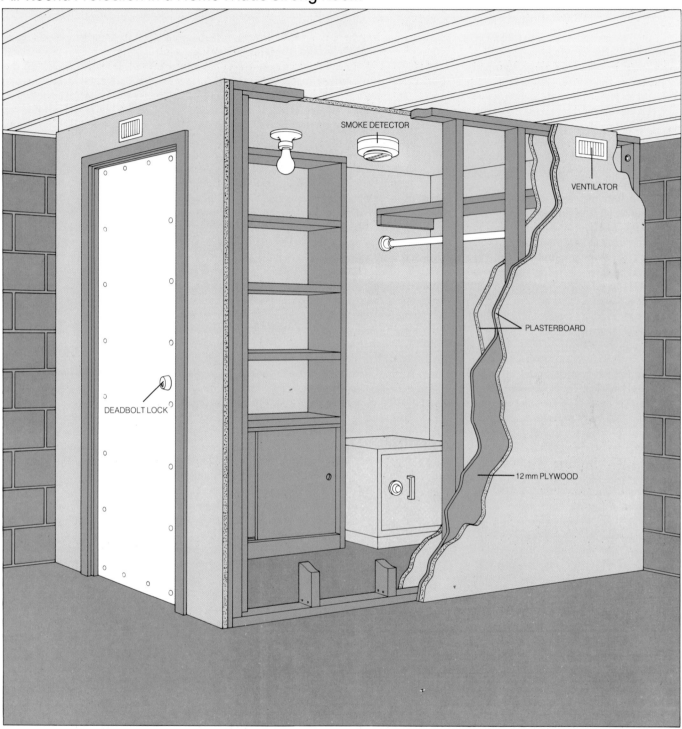

SMOKE DETECTOR

VENTILATOR

PLASTERBOARD

12 mm PLYWOOD

DEADBOLT LOCK

Building a strong room. For furs, camera equipment, guns, art objects and the like—and to provide extra protection for a safe—you can build a strong room from scratch in an unfinished basement *(above)* or alternatively you can convert an existing walk-in cupboard into a strong room. Cover the wall studs (working on the outside of a new room, the inside of an existing cupboard) with 12 mm plywood nailed every

150 mm. Add a layer of 12 mm special fire-resistant plasterboard, nailing it every 200 mm *(page 93)* and sheathe the ceiling and the other side of the studs with 12 mm plasterboard. Install a 44 mm solid-core wooden flush door that has been reinforced with a steel plate *(page 21)*, mounted to swing inwards on 100 mm hinges, and fitted with a good-quality deadbolt lock *(page 23)*. Frame holes in two of the walls and install

225 by 150 mm louvred ventilators to prevent moisture from collecting inside the room.

Add a light fitting and some detectors, inside and outside the room, wired to a centrally controlled alarm system *(pages 62–85)*. A pressure mat outside the room, a magnetic sensor on the door and a motion detector inside provide maximum burglar protection, while a smoke detector will alert you to the presence of a fire.

The Techniques for Welding Steel Grilles

Steel grilles are the traditional and most effective barriers for windows, but this effectiveness is offset by some disadvantages. Inside the house, grilles may block the light and view; outside they are visually obtrusive. For these reasons, grilles are generally used only on basement windows and windows that are hidden from sight. Even in such locations, you should consider leaving one window in each room unbarred, as a fire escape.

Window barriers come in three types. Ready-made, sliding grilles made of relatively light steel can be simply fixed inside the window *(page 54)*. With more labour, you can hire equipment and weld together a stronger, more attractive ornamental grille. Or you can bolt lengths of 12 mm flat steel horizontally over windows.

Welding—joining pieces of metal by heating them until they melt together—can be done in two ways. Gas welding, in which oxygen and acetylene are burned at the tip of a torch to melt the metal, is the traditional method, but for most D.I.Y. purposes it is quicker, safer and cheaper to use the process known as electric arc welding. Small arc welders that run off household electricity can be bought or hired.

In electric arc welding, an electric current jumps between an electrode and the metal, creating an arc of intense heat that melts both the electrode and the metal and forms a pool of molten weld metal. The secret of successful arc welding lies in applying the right amount of current to the right place for the right amount of time—an action called striking the arc. The arc is then moved away at a rate at which the weld metal solidifies in an even bead that penetrates the joint. The thickness of the metal you can weld is determined by how much current is available; a machine which is capable of producing up to 130 amps—the maximum current that can be used on a domestic 240 volt supply—is satisfactory for most workshop needs. Check

that your power supply is rated to provide sufficient current for the welding machine.

At all times it is necessary to take adequate safety precautions *(opposite page, above)*. The intensity of light and heat emitted cannot be over-emphasized. If you look directly at the arc without protection you will get arc flash, a painful condition akin to having sand rubbed in your eyes. You will need an arc-welding helmet or shield with a specially darkened lens, safety glasses with tinted lenses ("flash glasses"), gauntlet-style leather or fire-resistant gloves, and an apron made of leather or treated cotton that will resist hot metal and flying sparks.

The dramatic showers of sparks produced when welding make it necessary to work in an area protected against fire, such as a well-ventilated basement or garage with a concrete floor and masonry walls. If you have an exterior power supply you can work outside. Rest the metal to be welded on fire bricks laid on the floor or, if you intend to do a lot of welding, on a steel welding table to which the earth clamp can be attached.

The electrodes used in arc welding are metal rods coated with a chemical flux that shields the molten metal during welding from oxygen and nitrogen in the air, which might weaken the weld. The flux also mixes with the molten metal so that impurities float to the top of the weld, forming a coating of slag which must be chipped away after the weld cools *(page 49)*. The type of flux affects both the behaviour of the arc and how deeply the arc penetrates the workpiece, so you must check before starting work that you have the correct type and size of electrode for the metal you are working on. Too large an electrode will burn the base metal, while too small an electrode will be slow in forming a bead.

Electrodes are normally supplied either 300 or 400 mm long and in diameters ranging from 1.6 to 6 mm. They are classi-

fied according to their coating types, operating requirements and the mechanical properties of the deposited weld. In the U.K., for example, a typical steel electrode might be marked E4333R. The letter E shows that it is an electrode suitable for manual arc welding, the next four digits define the strength, and the final letter indicates the coating material. There may also be further optional digits and foreign classifications, so you should ask your supplier to advise you. Generally, buy an electrode with a core metal to match that of your work and a diameter to match the thickness of the metal you are working on.

All electrodes should come with specifications for the amperage range to use when welding with them. Mostly, the amperage increases with the thickness of the rod, but this can vary according to brand and rod composition.

Forming a good weld requires a lot of practice. The electrode must be correctly positioned or the weld will be out of place. If the arc is too long the weld will be erratic and metal droplets will splatter around the joint. Practise striking an arc and running a bead on clean metal scraps before you start working on expensive grille material, and familiarize yourself with the techniques used to make the basic joints shown on pages 48–50.

In the basic grille *(page 51)*, vertical pickets—steel bars 12 mm-square—fit through holes in two 25 by 6 mm horizontal bars called spreaders. Ask the steel supplier to punch evenly spaced picket holes in the spreaders, no more than 150 mm apart; if you plan to add ready-made ornaments, match the spacing to their width. Alternatively, if you have difficulty locating a supplier who can punch the holes, the bars can be laid across or abutted to the spreaders. You can cut the steel and grind the ends smooth with an angle grinder; otherwise ask the supplier to cut the bars to the required length.

A Safety Check List

☐ Never strike an arc, or look at it while you are working, without protecting your eyes by wearing a helmet or a welding shield. Do not allow people who are not protected or animals to come within sight of the arc.

☐ Always wear flash glasses. These not only protect your eyes from particles of slag but are also a safeguard in case an arc is struck accidentally.

☐ Protect your skin from the heat of the arc. Wear heavy gauntlets of leather or fire-resistant material and keep your collar buttoned and your sleeves rolled down. Clothes should ideally be made of leather or fire-resistant cotton, and free from grease and oil. Never wear synthetic fabrics.

☐ Spattered metal may catch in pockets unless they are buttoned down. For the same reason, do not wear trousers with turn-ups. Heavy boots that cover your ankles, or elastic-sided boots, are an additional safeguard.

☐ Never pick up recently welded metal with your bare hands; it will be very hot. Use tongs or pliers.

☐ Make certain your workplace is well ventilated. A portable fan gives extra ventilation when you are working on galvanized or zinc-coated steel which can give off toxic fumes.

☐ Do not keep combustible materials in the area or on your person at any time, and always have a fire extinguisher readily to hand. If a fire breaks out, unplug the machine before smothering the flames with the extinguisher.

☐ Keep your hands and clothes dry, and do not weld in a damp area.

☐ Inspect the equipment regularly. Do not use it if any of the connections are loose or if the insulation on any of the parts shows signs of wear.

☐ Make sure that you disconnect the equipment from the power supply whenever you are not using it and for cleaning, inspection or repair.

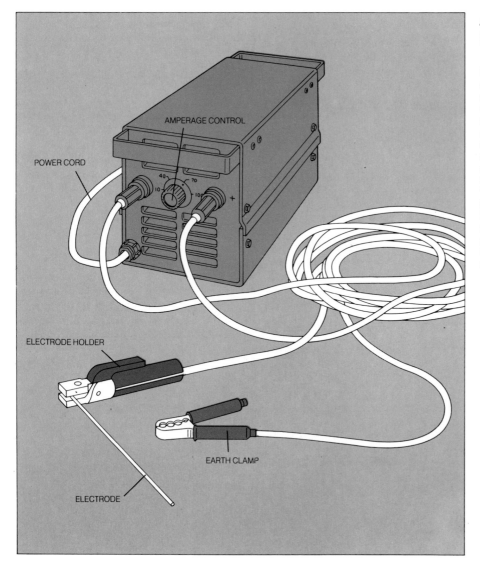

POWER CORD

AMPERAGE CONTROL

40 70
10 100
+

ELECTRODE HOLDER

EARTH CLAMP

ELECTRODE

Anatomy of a Portable Arc Welder

Safe pathways for the current. When the power cord of this welder is plugged into a 240 volt socket, a transformer inside reduces the voltage while increasing the amperage. The amperage is adjusted by turning a knob on the face of the machine. Two leads run from the machine, one carrying the earth clamp, the other carrying the electrode holder. In operation, the earth clamp is attached to the workpiece, the power is turned on and the electrode is held just above the metal. The current flows through the electrode holder into the electrode and jumps across to the metal, heating it to melting point, and then returns through the earth clamp to the transformer. Depending on its design, the earth clamp can be attached by spring jaws as shown on the left, a magnet or a screw thread.

Running a Straight Line of Weld Bead

1 **Striking an arc.** Set the amperage to 70, fasten the earth clamp to a piece of 6 mm mild steel scrap, then insert the bare end of a 2.5 mm general-purpose electrode into the electrode holder at an angle of 90 degrees. Switch on the machine. Making sure your arm is in a comfortable position, hold the tip of the electrode about 25 mm above the metal, then tilt the electrode at an angle of 15 degrees to the vertical. Put down the welding shield and sweep the electrode towards and on to the metal as if you were striking a match. As soon as the arc appears, lift the electrode about 2 mm away from the metal. Holding it perpendicular to the face of the metal, wait till a molten puddle appears at the tip, then pull the electrode away to break the arc.

Do not bring the rod into contact with the metal without a striking motion—the rod will stick to the metal. If this occurs, switch off the machine and loosen the rod by bending it gently from side to side. Make sure you do not damage the flux coating.

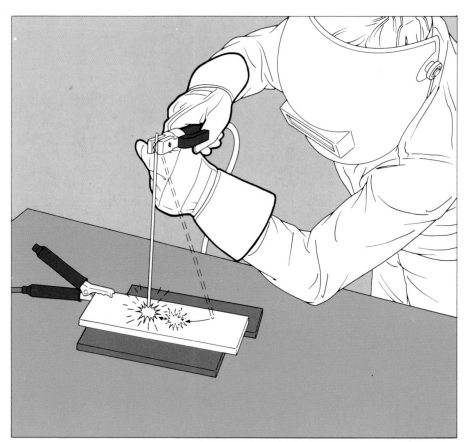

2 **Running a bead.** Strike an arc at one end of a scrap of 6 mm mild steel. When weld metal begins to form behind the molten puddle at the tip of the electrode, slant the electrode at an angle of 15 degrees to the vertical towards the direction of travel and move it slowly across the workpiece at a rate of about 50 mm per minute. You can tell if the electrode is the correct distance above the metal by listening to the sound it makes. If it is too close, it will make an irregular spluttering noise; too far and the arc will snap out. A steady crackling like frying bacon will tell you that the electrode is at the correct distance and moving at the correct speed.

As you move along and the electrode is melted down, keep applying a steady downward movement to ensure that the tip of the electrode is maintained at the correct distance from the workpiece. If the electrode is reduced to a 50 mm stub before you finish the weld, replace it with a new one. Before you resume welding, make sure you clean off all the slag *(opposite page, above)*. If you leave any and weld over it, it can weaken the joint. If you complete the weld before the electrode runs out, you must still clean off the slag.

To complete an interrupted bead, strike an arc 12 mm beyond the crater at the end of the bead *(inset)*. Move the electrode back over the crater, fusing the new weld metal with the old, then reverse it and continue in the original direction.

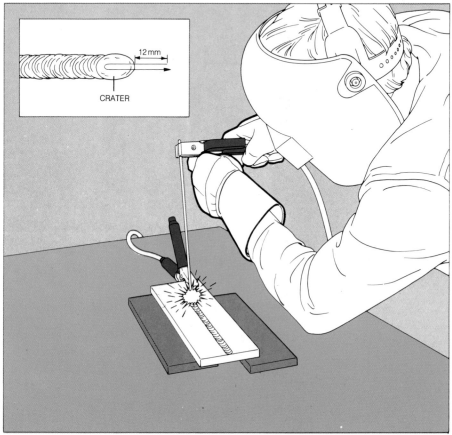

CRATER

12 mm

Slag Removal With a Hammer and Wire Brush

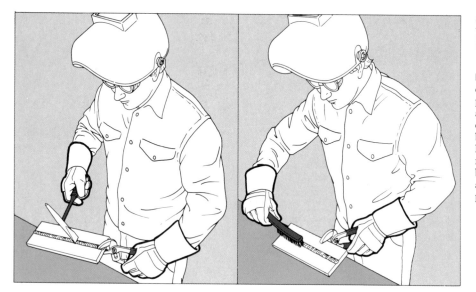

Removing slag. Wearing goggles to protect your eyes from flying lumps of hot slag, grip the hot piece of metal with pliers or tongs and strike along the weld bead with the square end of a chipping hammer to loosen the slag covering the bead *(far left)*. Then run the pointed end of the hammer along the junction of the bead and the metal to remove the slag. Finish off with a wire brush *(left)*. Scrub firmly up and down the bead and then across, to sweep away the remaining particles of slag.

How to Recognize a Solid Weld Bead

Judging a bead. Seen from above and in cross-section, these seven beads show the effect of the three main factors which influence a good weld: the current setting, the length of the arc and the speed at which the electrode travels. From the left, the first example shows an ideal bead: it has a smooth, rippling surface, and equal amounts of weld above and below the surface of the metal. The next two examples show the effects of an incorrect current setting—with too low a setting the bead does not penetrate, and with too high a setting the crater is over-large and spattered. In the fourth and fifth beads the length of the arc has been incorrect. If the arc is too short it produces a superficial bead; if it is too long, the bead will be shallow and spattered. The last two beads demonstrate how the speed at which the electrode is moved along affects the bead. Travel too slowly and there will be excessive waste metal, whereas too fast a rate creates a bead which is shallow and elongated.

The Two Basic Welds: Butt and Fillet Joints

Tacking a joint. To prevent the metal which is being joined from distorting under the heat of the arc, secure the two pieces temporarily with tack welds. Make the first tack weld at one end of the joint by striking an arc and holding the electrode in position for two to four seconds, depending on the thickness of the metal. Further tack welds should be made at intervals of 75 mm and at the opposite end of the joint.

When tacking a butt joint in metal more than 6 mm thick, first bevel both edges to an angle of 30 degrees with a bench grinder, then grind the bottom 2 mm of each to make them vertical *(inset)*. Make sure the metal is clean and smooth, then put the tacks in the bottom of the groove.

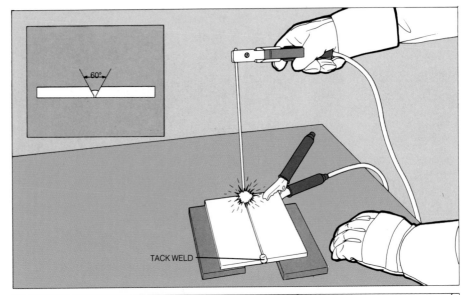

TACK WELD

Securing a butt joint. For metal less than 6 mm thick, use the method described on page 48 for running a bead of weld. Move the electrode at the correct speed so that it melts the full thickness of both pieces of metal *(top inset)*. If you go too fast the joint will not fuse completely; too slowly, and you will burn holes in the metal, leaving drips on the back. For metal thicker than 6 mm, weld in layers *(bottom inset)*. Make the root layer with the electrode almost touching the edges of the bevel, then clean this layer thoroughly *(page 49)* before going on to build up the others. Always clean each layer before putting down the next. When the weld is 1 mm above the surface of the metal, run a cover layer over the full width of the joint, making a slight weaving motion with the tip of the electrode. Using a pair of pliers, turn the metal over and check that the root layer has completely penetrated the joint. If it has not, clean the metal and make a light sealing run over the underside of the joint.

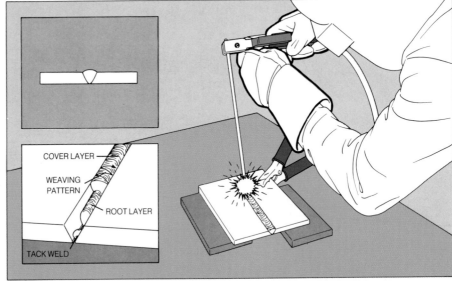

COVER LAYER
WEAVING PATTERN
ROOT LAYER
TACK WELD

Making a fillet joint. To avoid distortion, secure this joint with a series of welds on alternate sides. Divide the joint into 50 mm sections. Strike an arc and weld the first section on one side, then move to the other side of the joint and repeat the process on the next section. Continue in this way, alternating from side to side; slant the electrode at an angle of about 20 degrees in the direction of travel and keep the tip above the leading edge of the molten weldpool. The finished weld should have a triangular cross-section with sides of equal length, the depth of the weld—the throat—being equal to the thickness of the metal *(top inset)*. If you are cutting too far into the vertical face *(bottom inset)*, move the electrode closer to the horizontal and go more slowly, using a shorter arc. Once you have completed the alternating sequence, clean the metal and fill in the unwelded sections each side.

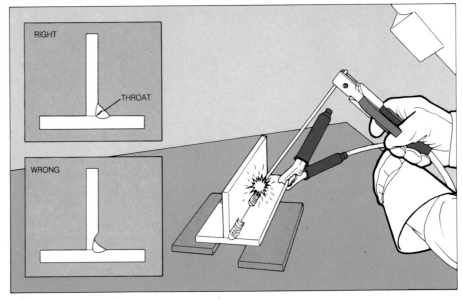

RIGHT
THROAT
WRONG

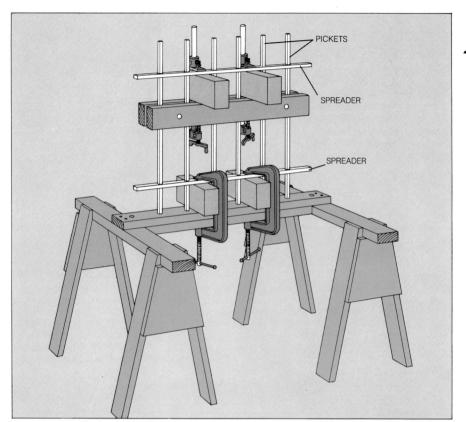

PICKETS

SPREADER

SPREADER

Welding a Simple Grille

1 **Making the jig.** To minimize the risk of distortion, assemble the grille in a home-made jig. Drill 15 mm holes, spaced for the pickets, in a 100 by 50 mm piece of hardwood; nail it to a slightly shorter piece of hardwood and then between two sawhorses. Hammer the pickets—12 mm-square steel bars the height of the window—into the drilled holes.

Set two firebricks on edge between two pairs of pickets. Slide a spreader—a 25 by 6 mm mild steel bar as long as the width of the grille, with 12 mm-square picket holes punched by the supplier—over the pickets, and then clamp the spreader to the pieces of hardwood.

Fasten two pieces of hardwood together loosely with coach bolts and slide this home-made clamp down around the pickets. Set two firebricks on the clamp, then slide another spreader over the pickets, and rest it on the firebricks. Get a helper to raise the assembly of hardwood clamp, firebricks and bottom spreader, and tighten the hardwood clamp when the spreader is level in its planned location—generally at the same distance from the ends of the pickets as the bottom one. Secure the spreader to the hardwood clamp with clamps. Check the angles of the pickets and spreaders with a steel square.

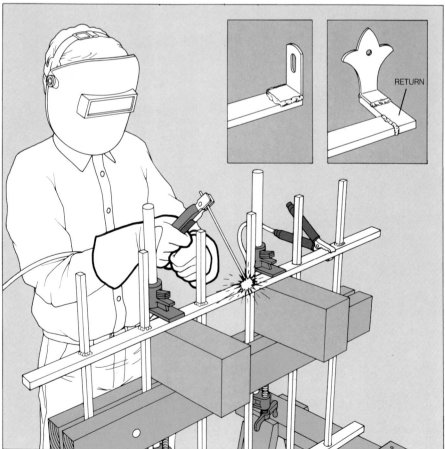

RETURN

2 **Welding spreaders to pickets.** Using a 2.5 mm electrode, weld round the pickets from above. Start at the corners and work your way in, checking for square as you go. Clean off all the slag, then release the grille from the jig and secure it again the other way up. Weld the pickets to the spreaders again from above—welding the joints on both sides of the spreaders minimizes the possibility of water penetration and rust formation. Repair any slight distortion by gently tapping the grille with a heavy hammer.

If you intend to bolt the grille inside a window recess *(page 54)*, hold narrow pre-drilled mounting clips (available from ornamental-iron suppliers) to the top of each spreader flush with the ends and weld them in place *(inset, far left)*. If the grille is being bolted to the face of a wall, weld a 75 by 30 by 6 mm piece of steel bar, called a return, to the end of each spreader and weld wider ornamental clips to the returns *(inset, left)*.

Twists and Turns
for Decorative Grilles

Twisting a picket. Using a picket as long as the height of the grille, clamp 150 mm of one end into a heavy-duty bench vice. To prevent the picket bending as it is twisted, slide a tightly fitting metal tube over the picket, leaving 150 mm uncovered. Choose a T-handle with a 6 mm-square hole (available from steel suppliers) and slide it on to the exposed end of the picket up against the metal tube. Rotate the T-handle, keeping it parallel to the sides of the vice and counting the number of turns, until the picket has the amount of twist you want and the ends line up squarely. If the picket does bend it can be straightened with a hammer and a V-block. Keep the number of blows to a minimum, as hammering will dent the spiralled edges on twisted metal.

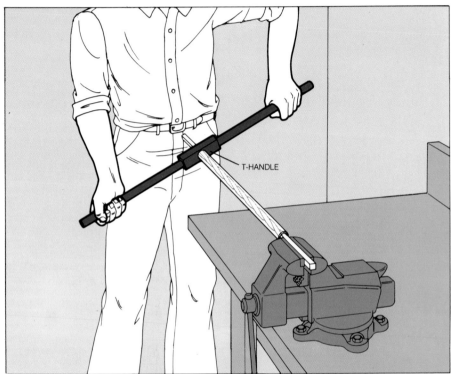

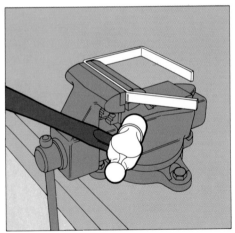

Making a diamond to fit between pickets. For a decorative diamond with equal sides, clamp a 12 by 3 mm steel bar in a vice. Bend the bar to a rough 90-degree angle by hand, then strike the bend with a ball-pein hammer until the corner is perfectly square. Bend the other sides of the diamond in the same way and cut off the extra length. Clamp the diamond closed and weld the ends together on the outer side of the joint.

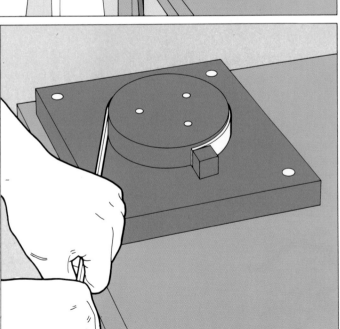

Bending a circle. To make a plywood jig for a circle, use a compass to draw a circle 6 mm smaller in diameter than the circle you want. Cut the circle out with a jigsaw, nail it to another piece of plywood and nail a small block of wood 3 mm from the circle. Slide the end of a 3 mm-thick steel bar between the circle and the block and bend the bar round the jig. Cut off the extra length of bar, clamp the circle closed and weld the ends together.

Forming scrolls. For an S scroll, draw on to 20 mm plywood a curve like the one on the right, with the help of the draughtsman's instrument called a French curve, making the notch 5 mm wide. Cut out the curve, glue and nail it to a piece of plywood and nail the assembly to a workbench. Bend one end of a 12 by 3 mm steel bar in a vice *(opposite page)* to fit the notch, slide it into the jig and bend the bar round the curve to make the upper part of the S; bend the other end of the bar round the jig to complete the S.

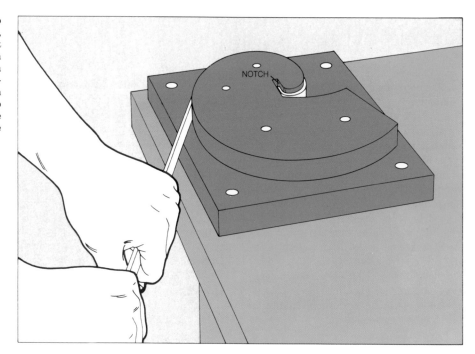

Window Grilles in a Choice of Styles

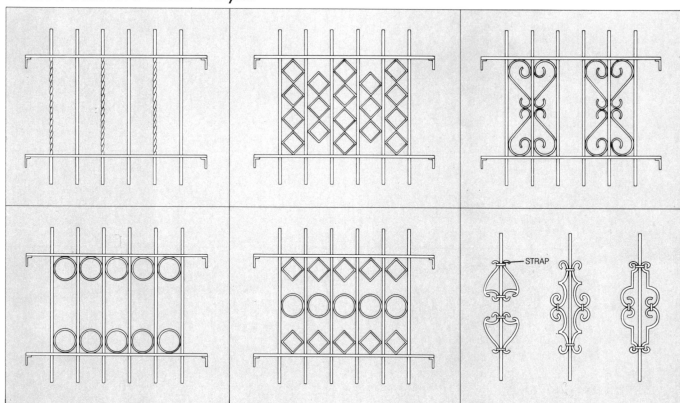

A choice of welded patterns. The grilles above vary in the complexity of their designs and welding procedures. In the simplest *(top left)*, twisted pickets alternate with straight ones, relieving the monotony of a plain grille. In the next four examples, ornaments are welded to the grille and to each other with butt joints on each side of the grille. Offset diamonds *(top centre)* create an unobtrusive visual screen for privacy. The rows of circles *(bottom left)* can be used to echo the curves of rounded architectural features, while the mixture of diamonds and circles *(bottom centre)* fits better with the angular lines of contemporary architecture. The scrolls *(top right)*, a more traditional motif, strengthen the grille with diagonal bracing. Three of the many prefabricated ornaments available from suppliers of ornamental iron are shown in the bottom right-hand drawing. The stirrup-like straps of these ornaments fit over a picket; the strap and the ornament are both welded on their inside edges to the picket.

Barriers of Steel for Vulnerable Windows

To increase security, many insurance companies recommend the fitting of external grilles to ground-floor and basement windows. Such grilles are usually made-to-measure; the choice is largely a matter of individual taste.

The sturdiest grilles are those which are secured by having extended spreaders set into the brick or block surround of the window *(below)*. In some models, the spreaders have detachable flanges that can be slid into the fixing holes after the grille is in place—this is a useful modification if the grille is particularly large and heavy. The surround should be at least 100 mm deep, and the brickwork should be in good condition, otherwise the grille may simply be jerked from its anchorage.

Alternatively, grilles may be bolted in place, either into the window reveal by means of mounting brackets welded to the spreaders *(page 51)* or directly to the face of the wall. In walls of solid masonry, use expanding anchors *(opposite page)* to secure the screws. The holding power of the anchors depends on the composition of the wall—concrete is strongest and brick is weakest—and on the tightness of pilot holes. In old, powdery masonry the bit size recommended by the anchor manufacturer may make too large a hole; experiment with smaller bits until you find one that bores a close-fitting hole.

To bore a pilot hole in solid concrete, you will need a hammer-action drill and a carbide bit. For a brick wall, use a drill with a masonry bit and locate the anchors deep in horizontal mortar joints—do not use the weaker vertical joints or the middle of a brick. The outside diameter of the anchor should match the thickness of the mortar joints between bricks (usually 9 mm). Avoid the type of anchor that is expanded by a hammer blow—the impact often crumbles the surrounding masonry.

When using any anchor, make sure the length and thread of the screw match those of the anchor. Stop tightening the fastener as soon as you begin to feel substantial resistance; over-tightening can cause the anchor to pull out entirely.

To prevent a burglar from removing the fasteners that hold a grille, alter the heads with a grinder *(page 38)*.

An External Window Grille

A grille set into a reveal. The vertical pickets of this steel window grille are slotted through horizontal spreaders and welded in place. The pickets have been cut to fit within the window reveal, but the spreaders are 100 mm wider than the opening to allow them to be set into the wall. The grille is simple to install. Mark the positions of the spreaders on one side of the window opening and drill holes 100 mm deep, using a 50 mm bit on a heavy-duty hammer-action drill. Enlarge the lip of the holes with a hammer and cold chisel. Drill holes 50 mm deep at the same level on the opposite side. Ease the spreaders on one side of the grille into the first set of holes, straighten the grille, and then slide the spreaders into the holes on the opposite side. Centre the grille so that the spreaders penetrate the brickwork to a depth of 50 mm either side of the window opening. Check the grille for square and cement the spreaders in position.

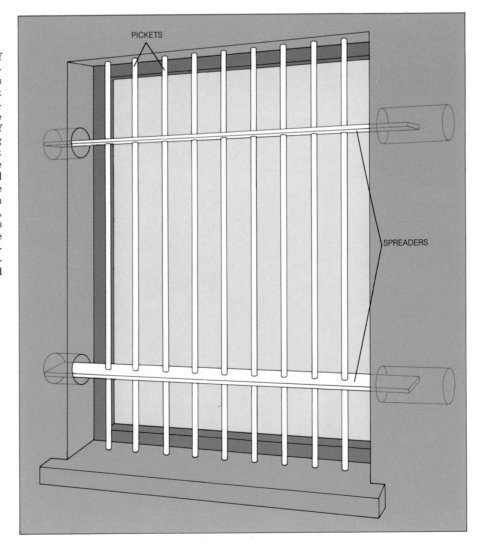

PICKETS

SPREADERS

Anchors for Masonry Walls

Threaded stud anchors. Designed for use with a machine nut and a washer, these anchors get their strength from especially deep pilot holes. The anchor on the right, above, tightens against the masonry when the nut forces a split sleeve over the mushroom-shaped end of the bolt. A few hammer blows tighten the anchor on the right, below, against the masonry by forcing the tapered pin into the split section of the shank; once tightened, the anchor cannot be removed.

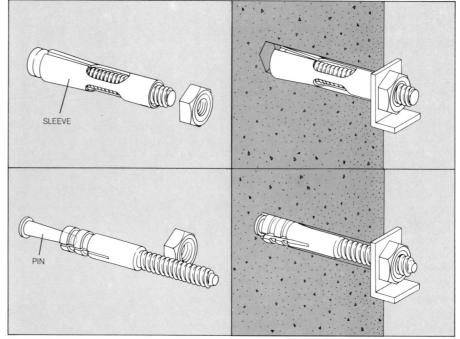

An expanding anchor. This anchor, suited to old or weak brick walls, is simply inserted into a snug pilot hole. As a machine screw or machine bolt is tightened, wedges at the ends of the anchor force the two sleeves apart, creating an even pressure along the entire length of the hole.

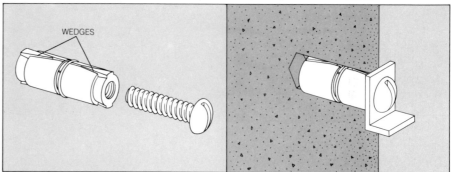

Anchors for concrete blocks. As the hollow-wall anchor *(right, above)* is tightened, the four leaves of the metal sleeve fold and expand against the inside of the block to lock the sleeve in place. The toggle bolt *(right, below)* provides excellent holding power in weak materials such as crumbly breeze block; the toggle unfolds in the space inside a block and is pulled back against the wall of the block as the bolt is tightened.

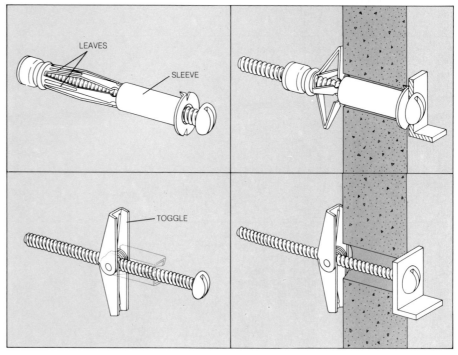

2

Silent Sentries, Loud Alarms

Electric alarm systems are more than a century old. Indeed, they predate the telephone, and Thomas Watson, Alexander Graham Bell's assistant in the invention of that ubiquitous instrument, acquired much of his considerable electrician's skill by installing alarms during the 1860s. One of the earliest alarm systems was patented in the United States in 1853 by Alexander Pope of Boston. Simpler than, but surprisingly similar to, modern electronic devices, Pope's invention consisted of pairs of electro-magnetic contacts mounted at doors and windows and connected with copper wire to a battery and a bell. When a window or door was disturbed and the contacts were separated, the bell rang. The chief drawback—the network could be easily defeated by cutting the wire—has been remedied in the best of today's alarm systems.

Those early devices, as well as later ones for detecting fire, were installed in offices and in the homes of the wealthy by protection services that also monitored the alarm systems. The same security can be purchased today; although it is expensive, you should bear in mind that most insurance companies will only approve professional installations by recognized security firms. Far less costly are alarms that you can install yourself to detect intruders, fire and, in sophisticated systems, a wide variety of other dangers.

The simplest of burglar alarms are not fundamentally different from Alexander Pope's invention. They employ a sensor for the door or window and use a battery to sound a buzzer. But unlike Pope's device, these alarms are self-contained, with battery, buzzer, wiring and, in most types, sensor for window or door all in one box. There are self-contained alarms for fire as well as for burglary and neither type requires more than a few screws to install *(pages 58–61)*. Yet there are limitations to these one-piece alarms. They sound off loudly when disturbed, but perhaps not enough to frighten a determined burglar who, in any case, may still be able to force open the door or window and silence the alarm.

Alarm systems with separate control panels for switching the sensors on and off generally suffer from neither of these faults. When a burglar opens a door or window fitted with sensors, the control box that serves as the brain of the system activates a siren or clangorous bell *(opposite)* that can arouse an entire neighbourhood; the alarm can only be silenced by switching off the system at the control box with a key. In many such systems, tampering with the alarm box beforehand—or cutting any of the wires in the system—will set off the alarm instead of deactivating the system. And some systems are designed to be connected to sensors that will alert your family to almost any danger, from a smashed window to a smouldering fire or a flooded basement.

Choosing a Simple but Effective Warning System

Smoke from a smouldering living-room sofa curls towards the landing while you and your family are upstairs in bed. Suddenly, an alarm blares from an inconspicuous fixture on the landing ceiling and, roused from sleep, everyone leaves the house quickly and safely.

A stranger approaches your house while you are away. Slipping to the side of the building, he starts to raise an unlocked window. A piercing alarm sounds out, and the would-be intruder hurries away.

Providing your home with such protection against fire and intrusion need not require an expensive, centrally controlled system and a maze of wires. Easily mounted, self-contained smoke detectors *(page 61)* give ample warning of a fire and, in a relatively low-crime area, inexpensive intrusion alarms may be adequate.

Operated by battery, and set on a door or window, an intrusion alarm will go off when the door or window is opened. The models shown here can be bought at department and hardware stores, and are especially useful for a limited number of entrance points.

The door alarm below is set simply by sliding the chain into place, while the type at the top of the opposite page is set with a removable key. Either kind should make enough noise to frighten off an intruder—and both can be primed to go off whether you are inside the house or not.

More sophisticated than any intrusion alarm are the so-called motion detectors, which are available in either mains or battery-operated versions. An ultrasonic detector *(page 60)* fills a "trap zone" inside a house with high-frequency sound waves which are inaudible to the human ear; the alarm is triggered when the wave pattern is disturbed by any movement. At the heart of a passive infra-red detector (PIR) is a sensor that will activate the alarm as soon as it picks up the body heat of an intruder *(page 78)*.

Unfortunately, all types of motion detector have certain drawbacks. Ultrasonic detectors can be activated by a strong breeze or vibration, or even by the ringing of a telephone or doorbell. In the case of PIR, the alarm can be set off by any new source of heat in the room, from a small animal to a burst of sunlight.

The false-alarm risk can be reduced by careful siting of the alarm *(page 60, below)*, and—in the case of ultrasonic detectors—by installing a unit with a tuning control, which allows the range to be adjusted. A relatively recent innovation is the dual-technology detector, which combines ultrasonic with PIR. In this model, the alarm will only go off after both sensors have been activated, so the chances of a false activation are greatly reduced.

Alarms for Doors and Windows

A door-chain alarm. Mount the alarm unit at the edge of the door, about 75 mm above the handle, and position the locking unit on the doorjamb to allow about 100 mm of slack when the door is closed and the chain block is at the end of the chain slot. When the alarm is set and the door is opened, the chain is pulled taut, causing the block to press against a switch at the side of the slot which activates the alarm.

The rotating lock cylinder on the doorjamb can be locked from both inside and outside, which allows the key-holder to enter and leave the house without tripping the alarm.

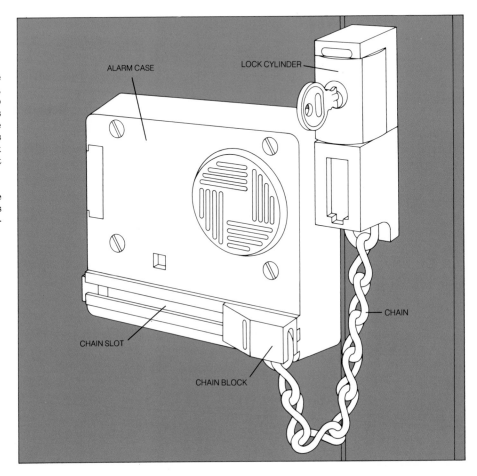

ALARM CASE

LOCK CYLINDER

CHAIN

CHAIN SLOT

CHAIN BLOCK

A key-switched door alarm. Mount the alarm unit at the edge of the door, about 160 mm above the handle. Secure the separate magnet to the doorjamb, aligning it with the reed switch of the alarm unit. The battery-powered alarm sounds when contact between the magnet on the door-jamb and the switch in the alarm unit is broken.

Because the unit is activated with a key, an intruder is unable to silence the alarm by switching it off. The unit has two settings—instant and delayed. With the switch at the instant position, the alarm will sound as soon as the door is opened, and will continue to sound until turned off with the key; closing the door will not stop the sound. With the switch at delayed, there is a pause of 25 to 30 seconds before the alarm sounds, giving an occupant time to leave or enter the house.

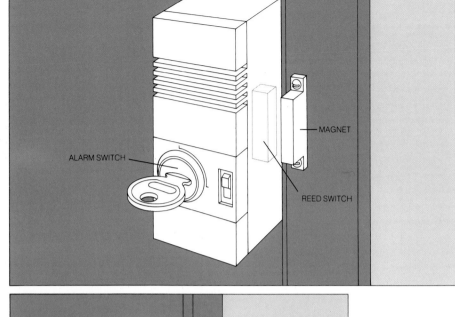

A portable alarm. Secure this small, battery-powered alarm to a window or door or to the side of the frame with double-sided adhesive tape or a hook. Plug one end of the lead into the alarm and wedge the metal prongs at the other end between the window sash or door and the frame. If an intruder attempts to open the window or door, the prongs spring apart and activate the alarm.

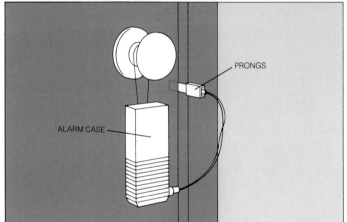

The Ultimate Alarm—a Family Dog

Perhaps the most reliable security system is a living one—the family dog. Extremely mobile, and requiring neither wires nor batteries, it can be trained to respond to most dangers or threats of danger. Almost any dog will raise an alarm in response to intrusion, but some breeds—Alsatians, Golden Retrievers and Dobermans, for example—make better watchdogs than others.

Whatever type you decide on, go to a reputable breeder and choose a friendly puppy that comes to you of its own accord when you are inspecting the litter. It should have bright eyes, a good appetite and a spot-free belly. It should also be inoculated against the usual canine diseases, especially parvo.

Once you have taken it home, an animal will need only obedience training and loving care to develop the combination of aggressive and submissive qualities that makes a good family watchdog. You can train a dog yourself at obedience classes, offered in many areas, or with the help of one of the many books on the subject. Audio and video cassettes are also available as training aids. A dog should start to give warning barks from the age of about four months.

Further training is unnecessary for family pets. Dogs that go beyond the sounding of an alarm signal to attack intruders are not recommended. A dog trained to bite any hand that holds a weapon or attack any suspicious person is generally advisable only for protecting commercial property.

An alternative to a live watchdog is an electronic one, which can be set to bark and growl like a dog when someone presses the doorbell.

Patrolling With Silent Sound

An ultrasonic motion detector. High-frequency sound waves fan out in an elongated oval from the front of this battery-powered unit. The waves are reflected from objects in the protected area and a microprocessor inside the unit compares the signal received with the one sent. Any major difference, such as would be caused by the movement of an intruder, is picked up, and the siren sounds for 100 seconds.

A key turns the unit on and off, and there is a special delay feature which enables you to enter and leave the room without tripping the alarm. The ultrasonic "eye" can be adjusted for different areas and distances—its maximum range is around 8.5 metres—and a tuning switch allows you to increase or decrease the sensitivity of the detector. The degree of sensitivity is shown by indicator lights on the control panel. An arrow marks the level at which sensitivity to human intrusion starts: sensitivity increases below the arrow and decreases above it. Indicator lights also show if the unit is functioning correctly, if an intrusion has been attempted during your absence, and if the batteries are getting weak.

The key block can be removed from the main unit and wired to it for installation elsewhere—in a bedroom or by the front door, for example.

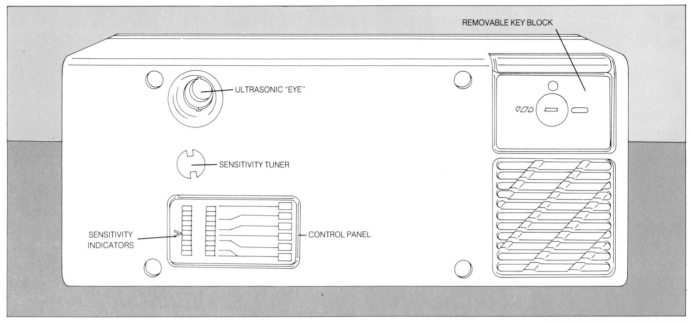

REMOVABLE KEY BLOCK

ULTRASONIC "EYE"

SENSITIVITY TUNER

SENSITIVITY INDICATORS

CONTROL PANEL

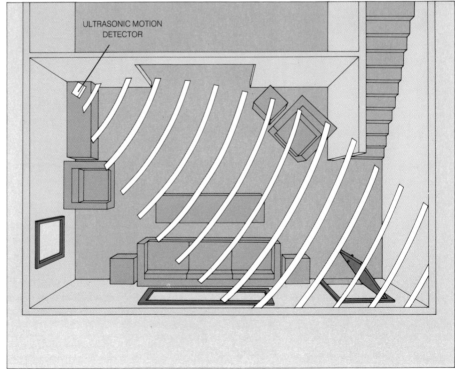

ULTRASONIC MOTION DETECTOR

Positioning an ultrasonic detector. Place the unit so that its pattern of sound waves covers entrances and exits, and so that an intruder could not move from the protected room to any other part of the house without tripping the alarm. To prevent false alarms, do not aim the pattern at a 90-degree angle towards vibrating surfaces, such as doors and windows, or towards sources of air movement, such as stairs and radiators.

Where to Put Smoke Detectors

No larger than many light fittings and easily fastened to any wall or ceiling, a smoke detector is the least expensive form of fire protection you can buy. Placed correctly, it sounds a warning early enough to enable you to escape from even a major fire. There are two basic types—ionization and photo-electric.

In an ionization chamber, a harmless amount of radioactive material causes electrically conductive particles to flow between two terminals, creating an electrical current. If smoke reaches the chamber, this interferes with the current and triggers the alarm. In a photo-electric detector, the alarm is tripped when smoke deflects a beam of light on to a light-sensitive switch.

The ionization smoke detector reacts more quickly to smoke from hot, fast-flaming fires, while the photo-electric type is quicker at detecting deep-seated, smouldering fires that produce heavy smoke and are commonly associated with burning furniture. You can buy double-system detectors which combine ionization and photo-electric devices in the one unit.

The placement of a smoke detector is critical. Since most fatal fires occur at night, detectors should be installed between the bedrooms and the potential sources of fire—the living room, dining room and kitchen. Detectors in other parts of the house *(right, above)* provide additional protection. Locations to avoid are kitchens, bathrooms and garages, where fumes or moisture could trigger a false alarm. Detectors should also be fixed well away from heaters, air-conditioning vents and, in the case of the photo-electric type, fluorescent lights. Always follow the manufacturer's instructions for installing and maintaining the unit.

Where two or more detectors are being installed, choose models that can be interconnected. Then, if one detector senses smoke, all the detectors will sound, giving a warning to everyone in the house.

The great majority of smoke detectors run on batteries, and so will continue to operate in the event of a power failure. Most detectors sound a warning bleep when the batteries start to run down. In general, batteries need to be changed about once a year.

Smoke detectors should be tested at least once a month. Most have a test alarm button; another test is to let the smoke from a snuffed-out candle drift over the unit. Occasional cleaning prevents build-ups of dust that could cause a detector to malfunction or to sound a false alarm.

Locating detectors in a house. Install at least one detector on every floor of a house. Set one in the centre of the downstairs hall or above the foot of the stairs, and protect sleeping areas with a detector in an adjoining hallway. Place additional detectors in the living room and dining room, which are both potential sources of fire, and also in any bedroom served by an electrical appliance such as an electric blanket or heater.

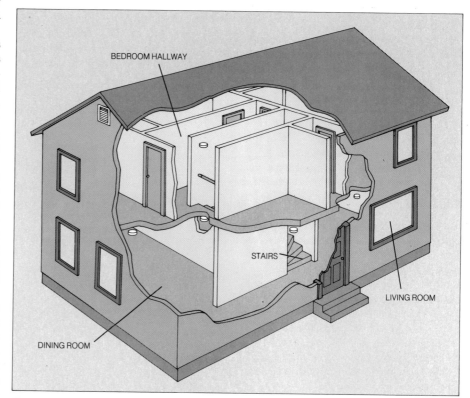

BEDROOM HALLWAY

STAIRS

LIVING ROOM

DINING ROOM

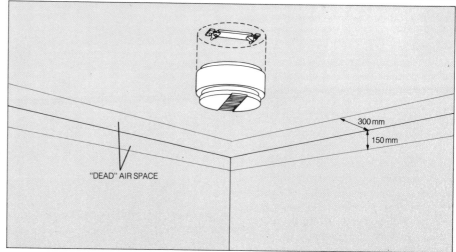

300 mm

150 mm

"DEAD" AIR SPACE

Locating a detector in a room. In most rooms, a ceiling-mounted detector should be at least 300 mm from any wall or light fitting—a central position is best. A wall-mounted unit should be between 150 and 300 mm below the ceiling. This is to avoid "dead" air spaces, in which the smoke from a fire is unlikely to circulate and a detector will be useless. On a ceiling with beams less than 100 mm deep, install the detector on the bottom of a beam, not in the space between the beams; if the beams are deeper, seek professional advice from a fire protection company.

A Network of Protection From a Central System

Anti-burglar protection for more than a room or two is best provided by a central system consisting of alarms and sensors linked to a control box by inexpensive, light-gauge wire. Such a system is more versatile and easier to maintain than several single-room alarms because it has one control box which can handle all the sensing devices needed to protect the whole house. A central system is also harder for an intruder to defeat because the alarms are located away from the sensors, and thus are not easy to track down and silence.

The brain of a central system is the control box, which continuously monitors the network of intrusion detectors mounted throughout the house. If a sensor trips, the message is relayed by the box to signalling devices—audible or visible alarms.

The control box contains terminals for connection to open and closed sensor circuits *(pages 64–65)* and to separate circuits for the external alarm, PIRs and panic buttons. A 24-hour circuit allows the alarm to be activated by a tamper circuit or panic button even when the rest of the system is switched off, and a timed entry-exit circuit allows the key-holder a period of time—usually between 10 and 60 seconds—to enter the house and switch off the system before the alarm sounds. The box has its own fuse and is tamper-proof.

The entire alarm system is switched on and off at the control box either by turning a key or by punching in a pre-selected code of digits in a key pad. Some sophisticated systems operate in zones, enabling you to switch on the sensors in some areas of the house while keeping other areas switched off. Power for the system comes from batteries that are recharged from the mains.

Simple control boxes are available as part of complete kit systems to which a large range of accessories can be fitted. These are sold in most department stores, electrical suppliers and D.I.Y. shops. Separate sensors, switches and control boxes can be bought from specialist security shops or from the manufacturers, but check that any accessories bought separately are compatible with the control box.

The control box can be mounted in any unobtrusive but accessible location, such as an understairs cupboard. Connections to alarms and sensors are made with insulated light-gauge multicore cable for 12 volt current; do not use solid core as this lacks the necessary flexibility. The cables can be snaked behind walls, hidden behind skirting boards, or even stapled in the open along walls or joists *(pages 66–71)*.

The numbers and types of sensors you need depend on the size and layout of your house. Intrusion detectors such as magnetic sensors and vibration detectors, or strips of metallic window tape, may be used to protect ground-floor windows and doors. Intrusion detectors may also be installed on any first-floor window that is easily reached—from a porch, garage or a climbable tree, for example. Wherever doors or windows are hidden in the back of the house or by shrubbery, providing concealment for a skilful burglar to disarm the sensor, you may want to add PIRs or pressure mats to your system *(pages 76–79)*.

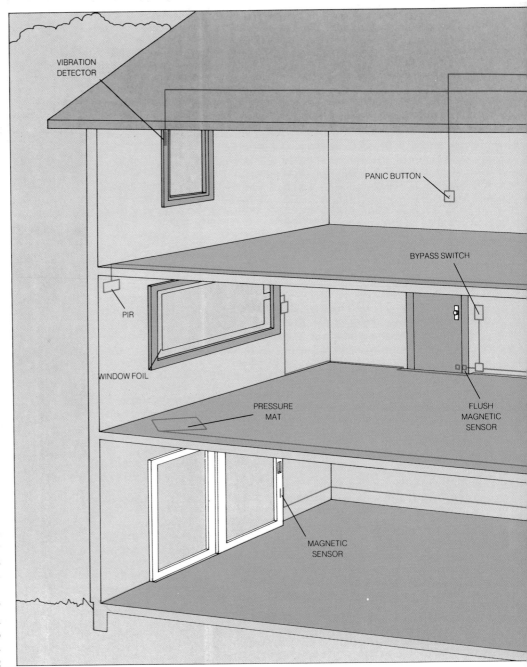

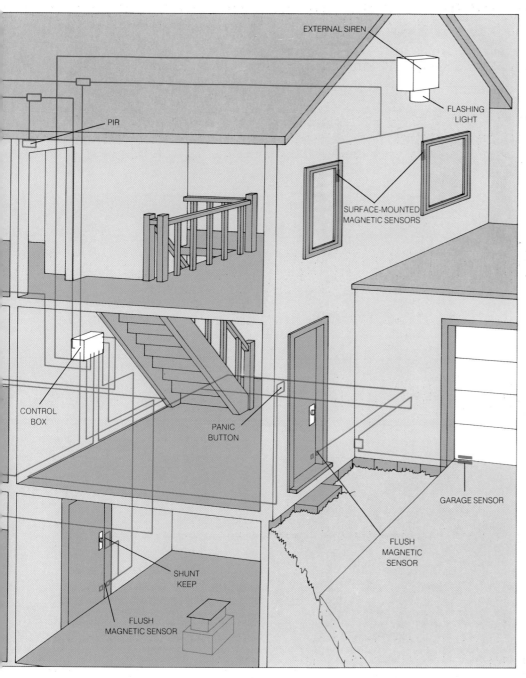

EXTERNAL SIREN

FLASHING LIGHT

PIR

SURFACE-MOUNTED MAGNETIC SENSORS

CONTROL BOX

PANIC BUTTON

GARAGE SENSOR

FLUSH MAGNETIC SENSOR

SHUNT KEEP

FLUSH MAGNETIC SENSOR

A central alarm system. In the house on the left, a control box mounted under the stairs is connected by cables to an array of strategically located intrusion detectors, signals and shunt (or bypass) switches. All accessible doors and windows are fitted with intrusion detectors, backed up by motion detectors in the living room and on the landing. A bypass switch to the living room door allows residents to pass through the doorway without having to switch off at the control box, and a pressure mat is located under the carpet. The door to the basement room containing an underfloor safe is fitted with a shunt keep, which combines the functions of a lock and a bypass switch. Panic buttons in the bedroom and beside the front door permit residents to sound the alarm manually if an intruder has managed to enter the house undetected. An alarm box with both siren and flashing light is mounted on the outside wall at the front of the house.

How Electronic Alarms Work: Two Basic Circuits

Wired alarm systems are triggered in one of two ways—by making an electrical connection or by breaking one. In the first type, the sensors interrupt the electrical path of the circuit so long as they are not tripped; the circuit is said to be open—no current flows—until an intruder trips a sensor and closes it. Then current passes through the system and triggers the alarm.

Because open circuits can be defeated simply by cutting a wire—so that tripping a sensor does not complete the circuit—they are seldom used to protect the perimeter of the house against intruders. Open circuits are most often used for pressure-mat motion detectors in relatively secure, interior locations.

In the second type of circuit, the electrical path is normally closed at every sensor and a small current flows constantly. When a sensor is tripped it breaks the circuit and a device in the control box reacts to the drop in voltage which touches off an alarm. In this system a break in a wire sets off the alarm.

In both kinds of circuit, a device in the control box makes it impossible to silence the signal merely by returning the sensor to the untripped position. This safeguard prevents a burglar from turning off the alarm simply by shutting a window or door he has just opened.

Certain types of sensors can be used only in one kind of circuit. And since you cannot mix open and closed sensors on the same circuit, you will need to buy a control box that can operate both kinds of circuit at the same time.

The Open Circuit

An open-circuit sensor. The pressure mat contains two thin sheets of metallic foil separated by perforated polyester foam *(below, top)* which prevents the flow of current. When the mat is stepped on *(below, centre)*, the conductors are pressed together, letting current flow to the control box to trigger an alarm.

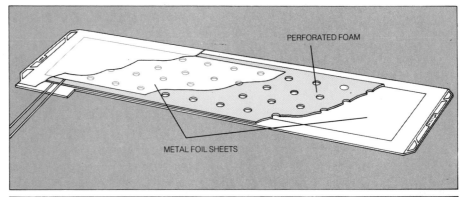

PERFORATED FOAM

METAL FOIL SHEETS

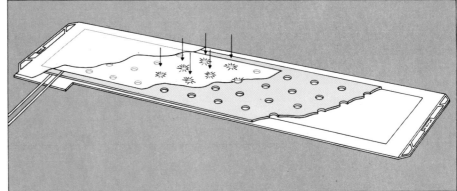

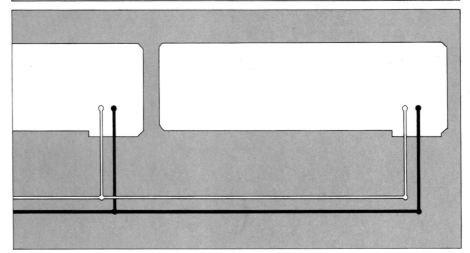

Wiring an open circuit. When more than one pressure mat is wired into an open circuit, they must be linked together in a pattern called parallel wiring. Each sensor wire in the cable leading from the control box is attached with a soldered connection *(page 77)* to a separate wire from the pressure mat, then runs to the corresponding wire on the next mat *(above)*. As many pressure mats as necessary can be added to the system in the same way.

The Closed Circuit

A closed-circuit sensor. This magnetic door sensor consists of two parts: a magnet fitted to the door, and a reed switch mounted on the frame *(below, left)*. The reed switch consists of two metal contacts sealed in a vacuum inside a glass phial. When the door is closed and the magnet is near the switch, the contacts are pulled together, allowing a small current to flow in a continuous loop through the circuit. When the door is opened *(below, right)* the magnet moves away from the switch and the contacts are parted, interrupting the flow of current and triggering the alarm.

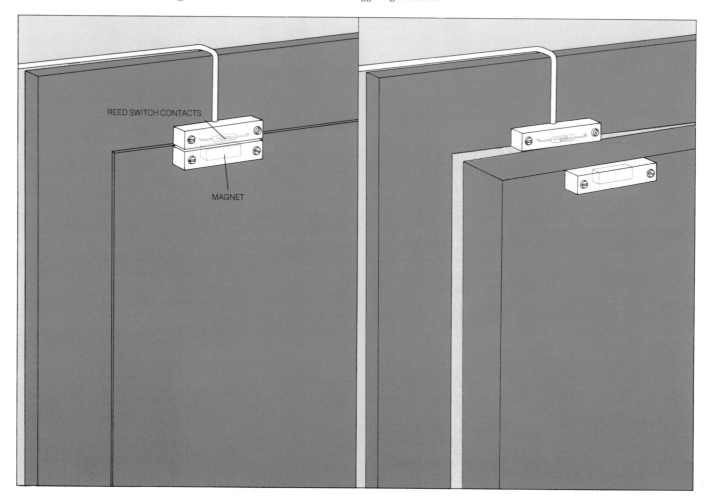

REED SWITCH CONTACTS

MAGNET

Wiring a closed circuit. When more than one sensor is wired into a closed circuit, the sensors must be linked in a pattern of series wiring. One wire from the two-core cable leading from the control box runs to one of the two reed switch terminals on the first sensor; a separate wire runs from the second reed switch terminal to the first terminal on the next sensor. This pattern is continued up to the last sensor in the series. The second wire from the two-core cable runs to one of the three spare terminals on the first sensor; a separate wire runs to a spare terminal on the next sensor, and so on as far as the final sensor in the series, where the separate wire is run to the second reed switch terminal.

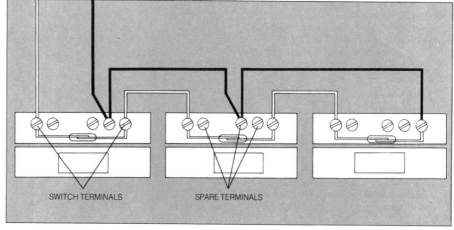

SWITCH TERMINALS   SPARE TERMINALS

How to Snake Cables Through the House

Because there is little danger of shock or fire from the low-voltage wiring used for alarm systems, the cables linking the various sensors around the house to the central control box are light and flexible and they need not be installed according to the rigorous regulations that govern ordinary house wiring. They can be laid anywhere except within 225 mm of house wiring, or near sources of heat—tucked under carpets, hidden behind mouldings, passed behind skirting boards. Wherever possible, avoid running the cable across walls where people could drive picture hooks through it.

The easiest wiring route for an alarm sensor or switch is in an unfinished attic or basement, where exposed cables can be simply secured to joists or wall surfaces with cable clips or insulated staples. The best time to lay concealed cables in rooms is when you are redecorating—you can then cut channels for cables in walls or remove skirting boards without worrying too much about the mess. In every house, however, there are a number of possible routes for concealed cables that involve very little disturbance to surface decoration.

For vertical runs—for example, to get cables from a basement or attic to other floors—you may be able to drop the cable behind the plasterboard of a timber-frame wall *(opposite page)*. The excess space alongside a boxed-in internal plumbing stack and built-in cupboards on successive floors provide two more excellent routes *(page 68)*. If cupboards are located directly over each other, simply drill up through the ceiling of one into the floor of the next. If they are offset, you may be able to fish cable a short distance through a joist space shared by the cupboards; alternatively, you can run the cable out of the top of a lower cupboard to a moulding, then into the bottom of the upper cupboard.

Horizontal runs of cable can be concealed under the edges of wall-to-wall carpets or behind skirting boards *(page 69)*. If you hide cable under rugs or carpet, avoid places where the insulation could be damaged or the wires broken by foot traffic or heavy furniture. When running cable for pressure mats under a stair carpet, drill channels through the stair nosings to protect the cable *(page 71)*.

Although tongue and groove floorboards are difficult to take up, face-nailed boards can be lifted with relative ease to enable you to pass cable under the flooring *(page 70)*. The tools you will need include the lid of a length of PVC trunking for passing the cable under the floorboards; a straightened wire coathanger, which makes a handy tool for poking a path through packed insulation and for "fishing" a cable over a short distance; a flat wood bit for drilling through joists; and a cold chisel and club hammer for cutting a channel behind skirting at the sides of the room. Avoid making any connections between cables under the floor where it will be difficult to check for faults in the wiring.

Most sensors require two-core, multi-strand cable, but check with the manufacturer's instructions. Vibration detectors, bypass switches, shunt locks and shunt keeps will require four or six-core cable, and for passive infra-red motion detectors you will need six or eight-core cable. Do not use cheaper solid conductor cable, which is less flexible than the multi-strand type and liable to break when being routed through the house.

When estimating the length of a run, add an extra 300 mm for each connection and buy 20 per cent more than the total estimate, since the cables will rarely run in a straight path. If you need a large amount of cable, check with your electrical supplier whether a 100-metre drum could be a more economical purchase.

Hanging the control box. On an understairs wall or in a similar inconspicuous but accessible place, use a spirit level to mark a horizontal line for the bottom of the box. Remove the front of the box or open the cover. According to the design, mark fixing holes through the back of the box while a helper holds it in position or mark the positions of the hanging brackets. Drill and plug the fixing holes. While a helper supports the box, and checks for level, secure it to the wall with the screws provided *(right)*. When sensor and alarm circuits have been connected to the control box terminals and tested *(pages 84–85)*, get a qualified electrician to connect the box to the mains.

Wiring From an Attic Through a Stud Wall

1 **Drilling through the head plate.** In the attic, locate the top of a stud wall by tapping along the attic flooring, and drill down into it through the head plate. Near the bottom of the wall, underneath the attic, drill a hole through the plasterboard for the cable exit *(right)*. Knock the face of the wall between the two drilled holes to determine the location of any horizontal noggings between the studs. Where you find a nogging, drill through the plasterboard immediately above and below the nogging, then chisel out a channel in the plasterboard between the holes.

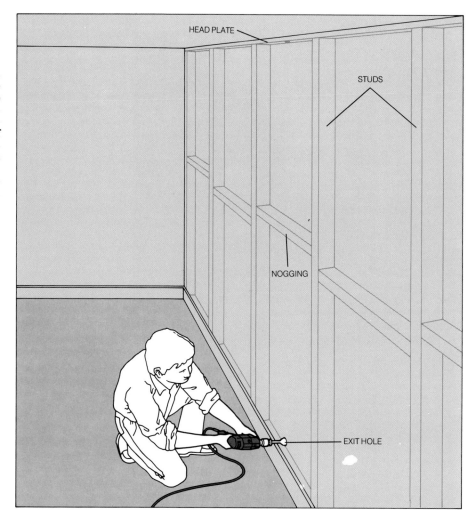

2 **"Fishing" the cable.** Attach a weight, called a "mouse", to one end of a long piece of string and tie the other end to the cable. Stagger the points of attachment to avoid a bulky connection *(inset)*. Drop the mouse through the hole in the head plate. If there are noggings behind the plasterboard, fish out the mouse through the hole drilled above the nogging, then drop it back behind the plasterboard through the hole below the nogging. Pull the mouse and its string through the exit hole and draw the cable through behind it with a hooked length of stiff wire such as an old coathanger. Disconnect the mouse and the string. Make sure the cable is lying flat in channels cut into the plasterboard over noggings, and then plaster over the channels to a smooth finish.

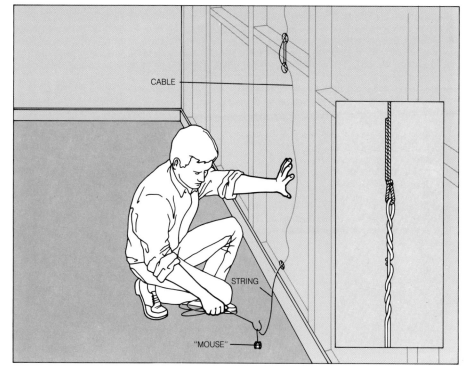

Two Routes for Vertical Wiring

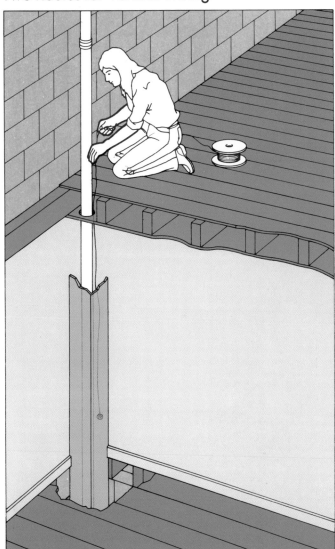

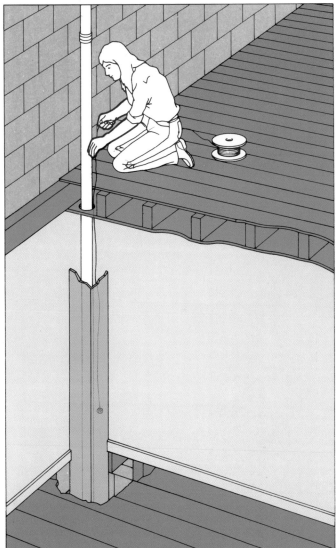

Running cable along a soil stack. Kneeling on the attic floorboards or on a board laid across the joists, feed a mouse attached to a length of string and the end of the cable *(page 67, below)* into the gap between the boxing and the pipe. If the weight catches, jiggle it around so that it passes the obstruction. Drill an exit hole lower down the boxing, pull out the mouse, and draw the cable down the inside of the boxing.

If you are running cable from a room below the attic, drill an access hole in the boxing and feed the string and cable through in the same way.

Running cables through cupboards. When cupboards are not located directly above one another, run cables from the lower floor through a hole drilled in the floor of a cupboard above. Drill a hole through the lower cupboard ceiling and into the space between the joists above, then drill a hole down into the same joist space through the floor of a cupboard on the next floor, and feed a length of heavy string, secured to the floor with a nail, into the hole. Push a piece of hooked wire towards the string from the lower cupboard *(inset)*. Twist the wire to snag the string, pull it back to the lower cupboard, tie the string to the cables and pull them into the upper cupboard. Drill through the ceiling of the upper cupboard and into the attic. Pull extra wire into each cupboard and staple it neatly to the wall.

If the cupboards do not share a joist space, remove a section of skirting board in the upper room and drill behind it at an angle into the joist space above the lower cupboard. Run the cables through the drilled hole and behind the skirting *(opposite page)* to the nearest cupboard or sensor.

Concealing Cable in a Solid Wall

Chasing a channel. Hold a length of 12 mm oval plastic conduit against the wall along the planned cable run and mark along its sides. With a bolster and club hammer, chip out a channel between the marked lines about 6 mm deeper than the thickness of the conduit. Use a cold chisel for removing the plaster behind obstacles such as picture rails. Thread the cable through the conduit, then lay the conduit in the channel and secure it to the wall with either cable clips or insulated staples placed every 300 mm. Plaster over the channel to a smooth finish.

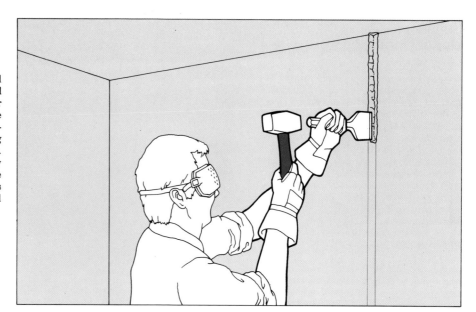

Concealing Horizontal Wiring

Hiding cables behind skirting boards. Starting at one end of the wall, prise the skirting board away from the wall with an old wood chisel and insert wooden wedges into the gap. Continue along the wall until the entire skirting board has been removed. Push the cable into the gap between the floor and the bottom of the plaster or plasterboard; if there is no gap, cut a groove along the wall using a trimming knife to cut away plasterboard, and using a club hammer and cold chisel for plaster. Nail the skirting back in place, angling the nails to avoid the cables.

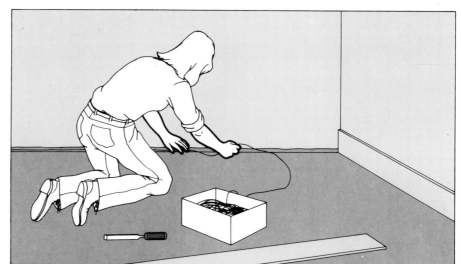

Wiring under a carpet. Use a screwdriver to lift the edge of carpet secured with spiked gripper rods, then fold back both the carpet and underlay and lay the cable along the room side of the grippers. Tack the cable to the floor with insulated staples at intervals of 300 mm. Fold back the underlay on top of the cable and stretch the carpet back on to the grippers; use a bolster or piece of wood to push the carpet edge down into the gap between the grippers and the skirting.

If the carpet is secured with double-sided adhesive tape, you may be able to lay cable under the carpet in the gap between the tape and the wall or skirting.

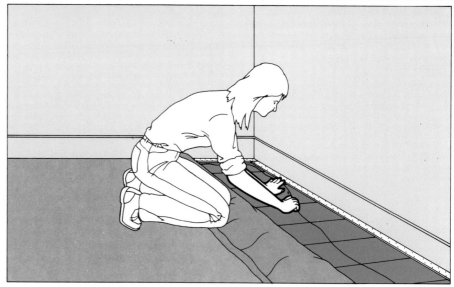

Running Cable Under Floorboards

1 Crossing the room. To run cable parallel to the joists, use a bolster to lever up one floorboard at each end of the room; if the boards are tongue and groove, cut off the tongue of the board being removed. Leave any boards directly under skirting boards in position. Attach the cable to one end of the lid of a length of 18 mm plastic trunking, long enough to span the room; push the lid into the gap left by one of the lifted boards and push it under the floorboards between joists. Whip the lid round any obstacles. At the opposite side of the room, pull out the lid with the attached cable from under the boards *(right)*; detach the cable. Make sure the cable lies well away from any underfloor mains cable.

To run cable across the joists *(inset)*, lift a floorboard and, with a flat wood bit, drill a hole through each joist; the holes should be at least 100 mm below the top of the joists to prevent nails penetrating the cable when the floorboards are replaced. Feed the cable through the holes, taking care not to pull it too taut.

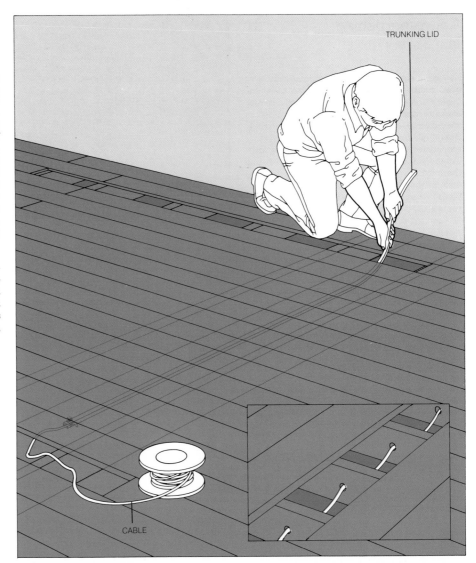

TRUNKING LID

CABLE

2 Fishing out the cable. Use a cold chisel and club hammer to chip out a channel in the wall adjacent to the floorboards. Take hold of the cable end with one hand and, reaching under the floorboards, push it towards the channel in the wall; with your other hand, draw the cable up through the channel, using a hooked piece of wire if necessary. Replace the floorboards.

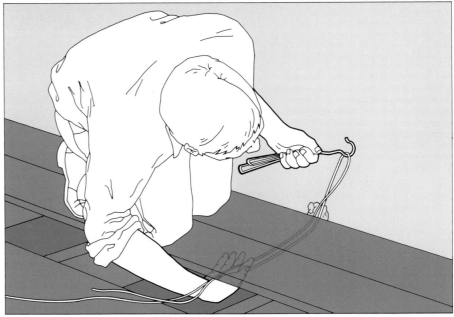

A Channel Behind the Skirting

Pulling up the cable. If the room is papered, dampen a small section at the corner where the skirting board meets the doorjamb and carefully peel back the paper. Using a cold chisel, make a recess about 25 mm square in the plaster at the corner, then chip out a channel behind the skirting. Drill a small hole through the skirting at the bottom of the channel. Run the cable under the carpet up to the doorjamb *(page 69)*. Push the end of the cable into the hole and up the channel, then pull it through behind the skirting *(right)*. After connecting the cable wires to a door sensor *(page 73)* or junction box, make good the plaster and replace the paper.

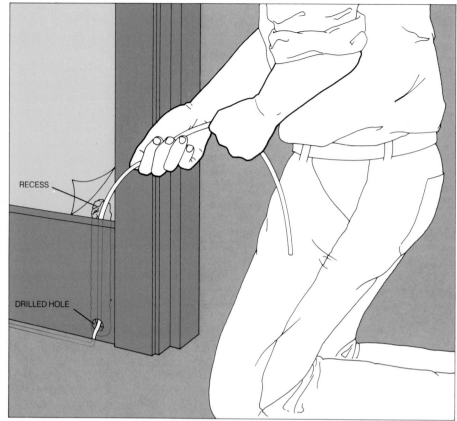

RECESS

DRILLED HOLE

Wiring for Pressure Mats on Stairs

Threading cable through stair nosings. Plan the route of the cable to run as near the edge of the carpet as possible. Lift the carpet and drill a 6 mm hole at an angle through the nosing of each step the cable is to cross. If the gripper rods extend across the full width of the carpet, chisel out a small channel in the treads and risers behind each gripper *(inset)*. Pass the cable through all the holes and channels to the pressure mat, tacking it to the treads with insulated staples or cable clips. Replace the underlay and carpet.

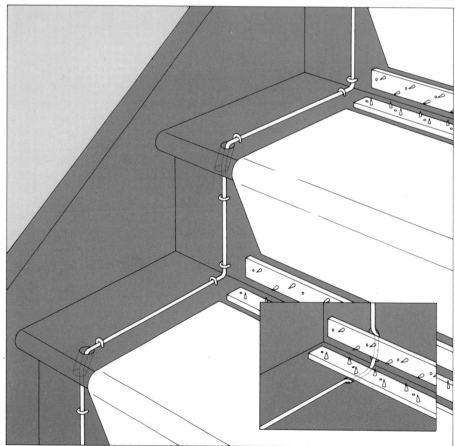

Sensors: the Eyes and Ears That Detect Trouble

A versatile centrally controlled alarm system requires a variety of sensors, detection devices that signal the control box when something is amiss—when a window or door has been opened, or someone is moving around inside the house. For each of these dangers and many others, there are several types of sensor.

Most central alarm systems are installed primarily to warn of intruders, and the sooner your system detects them, the better. First protect the "perimeter" with sensors at exterior doors and windows which are accessible from the ground or next to a porch or balcony. Once the perimeter is secure, you may want additional sensors to detect a burglar who breaches the perimeter and manages to get inside the house *(pages 77–78)*.

For the perimeter, the most popular sensor is a two-piece magnetic type: a magnetically tripped reed switch for the frame and a magnet for the door or window *(opposite page)*. The magnet holds the switch closed; when the door or window is opened, the magnet moves and trips the switch *(page 65)*. For doors and casement windows, attach magnetic sensors near the unhinged side, so that the alarm will sound at the slightest opening. On external windows and doors, cover exposed terminals by plastering them with epoxy putty or mineral insulating compound before screwing the sensor in position.

Magnetic sensors are manufactured in models that can be recessed for concealment or, more simply, screwed to structural surfaces. The surface-mounted type is generally used for metal windows, because it is not practical to drill the large hole required for a recessed sensor in a metal frame. Anodized versions are available for fitting on patio doors, and a special sensor is available for such applications as garage doors, where the switch and the magnet may be spaced more than 6 mm apart.

Although magnetic sensors are the type most commonly used for perimeter protection, other sorts are used in special situations—on out-of-the-way windows for instance, where an intruder can gain easy access if he smashes or cuts the glass. For fixed glazing such as picture windows, the least expensive solution is a strip of foil glued round the perimeter of the glass *(pages 74–75)*. The foil tears when the glass is broken and triggers an alarm. Take great care not to scratch or tear the foil during installation or subsequent maintenance and window cleaning.

More sophisticated protection is provided by vibration detectors, which guard doors and windows by detecting the shock patterns of a forced entry *(page 76)*. This allows windows to be partially locked open for ventilation without any loss of security, provided the gap is not greater than 125 mm. Choose an electronic type, incorporating a light-emitting diode to identify the tripped sensor. They are secured to the frame of the window and are individually adjusted once they have been installed.

Inside the house, the presence of an intruder can be detected in several ways. Pressure mats set off the alarm if someone treads on them *(page 77)*. These should be located under the carpet near doors and prime targets such as hi-fi equipment and video recorders. On stairs, position two narrow mats on consecutive treads.

Motion detectors guard whole rooms rather than specific danger points. Some work on the same principle as radar, sending out high-frequency radio or sound waves; if the frequency of the beam is distorted the alarm is set off. Passive infrared detectors (PIR) cover a fan-shaped area and respond to changes in infra-red energy within that zone *(page 78)*. Position these to avoid possible sources of false alarms such as hot sunlight on a window, fires or radiators; some models are specially designed not to react to pets.

As a last line of defence there are panic buttons, which are wired into a 24-hour circuit and so allow you to activate the alarm even when the rest of the system is switched off. They latch mechanically when depressed and can only be released with a key. Panic buttons can be either wall mounted or flush mounted into a standard electrical box *(page 79)*.

Before installing any part of the alarm system, carry out a bench test on the control unit and the external alarm. Once you are satisfied that they work, test each sensor to save the trouble of tracing a fault once the system is installed. Motion and vibration detectors have an integral test light, but for simpler sensors you should use a continuity tester, available from most electrical suppliers. For magnetic sensors, place the magnet near the sensor and touch the sensor switch terminals with the tester probes—the light in the tester should come on, only going out if the magnet is removed. For pressure mats, touch the probes to the stripped alarm wires—the tester light should come on only if the mat is stepped on. After installing the whole system, test each sensor again, while a helper stands by at the control unit.

When wiring up the system, choose a colour code for the individual wires within the cables, to differentiate between their functions. Stick to this code throughout the entire installation, to prevent mixing the wires. Code the cables themselves in the same way, using different coloured adhesive tape, so that at the end of the installation you will know which cable in the control box corresponds to which sensor.

A Flush-Mounted Sensor

Recessing the sensor for a door. Chisel a recess in the corner of the wall just above the skirting board and route the cable from the control box to the doorjamb *(page 71, above)*. Using a spade bit the same diameter as the sensor, drill a hole in the jamb at the same height as the recess, and slightly deeper than the switch to allow for slack in the cable. Mark and chisel a recess for the face plate. Drill through the jamb to connect the sensor hole and the recess in the wall, then push the cable through the jamb and attach the wires to the terminals at the back of the sensor switch *(right)*. Slide the sensor in position and screw it to the jamb, twisting the cable in a clockwise direction to form a coil with the slack. Drill and chisel a recess for the magnet in the closing edge of the door, aligning it exactly with the sensor *(inset)*, and screw the magnet in place.

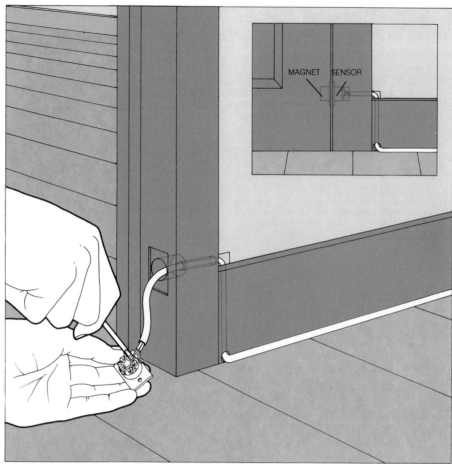

A Surface-Mounted Sensor

Mounting the sensor on a window. Connect the cable to the terminals on the back of the sensor. Hold the sensor against the window frame and mark the position of the screw holes; drill pilot holes and then secure the sensor to the frame with the screws provided. Hold the magnet on the sash, aligning it with the sensor on the frame, and secure it in the same way.

For the top sash of a sliding sash window, mount the sensor on a short piece of wood near the top of the inner sash channel to make it level with the magnet. To protect the lower sash, mount the sensor on the staff bead, the strip of moulding that holds the sash in its channel. On a patio door, install the sensor and magnet at a height where they will not be knocked or damaged by the feet of people passing by.

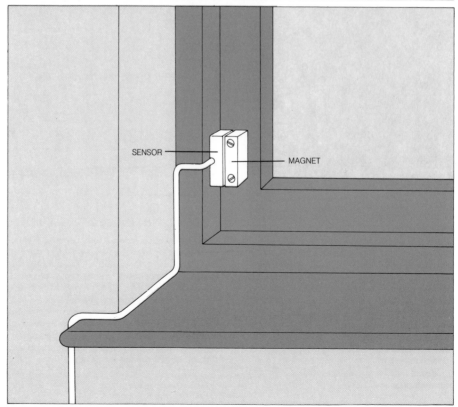

A Heavy-Duty Sensor for the Garage

Wiring to a junction box. A few millimetres inside the garage door, drill and plug screw holes in the floor for the pre-wired sensor, then secure the sensor with 37 mm stainless steel screws. On the inside face of the garage door, align the magnet with the sensor and screw it to the door; use self-tapping screws or screws and nuts for metal doors. Secure a junction box terminal plate to the inside wall of the garage adjacent to the door and run a four-core cable from the control box to the junction box. Following your colour-coding arrangement for sensor and tamper wires, connect the wires from the control box cable and from the sensor cable to the terminals in the junction box. Screw on the lid of the junction box.

JUNCTION BOX

MAGNET   SENSOR

Strips of Foil to Signal Window Breakage

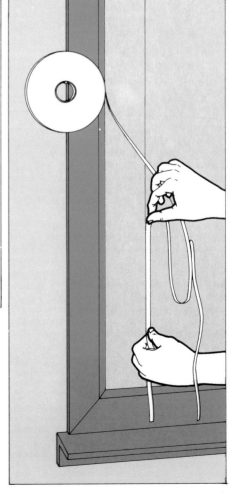

1 **Laying out the foil pattern.** For a window that does not open, such as a picture window, use a wax pencil and a piece of wood or stiff cardboard 75 mm wide to lay out a route for the foil. Working on the outside, start the pattern at the bottom of the window, using the width of the cardboard to draw a line 75 mm from the window frame. Continue round the window to complete the pattern shown in the inset. The beginning and the end of the pattern should be 40 to 75 mm apart.

Clean the inside of the glass with alcohol and allow it to dry thoroughly.

2 **Applying adhesive-backed foil.** Leaving 50 mm of foil hanging over the window frame, start at one end of the pattern and stick the foil to the inside of the window along the wax-pencil marks on the outside. To do so, peel a few centimetres of backing paper from the tape—hang the roll of foil from a nail near the window for convenience—stretch it tight and press it against the glass *(right)*. Smooth any bumps or wrinkles with a piece of thin cardboard. If the foil tears, remove it and start again.

3 **Turning a corner.** At a corner, double the foil back on itself and crease it gently along the intersecting line *(below, left)*. Start the foil along the wax-pencil line in the new direction, making a second crease in the corner at a 45-degree angle *(below, right)*. Smooth the foil at the corner with a piece of thin cardboard and continue to apply the foil around the window, stretching it taut and smoothing it flat as you go. Leave a 50 mm tail of foil at the end of the run.

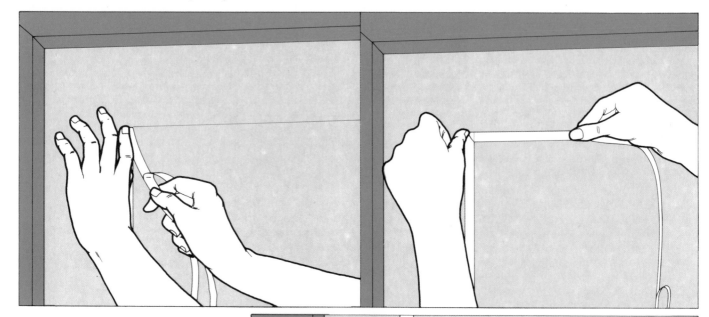

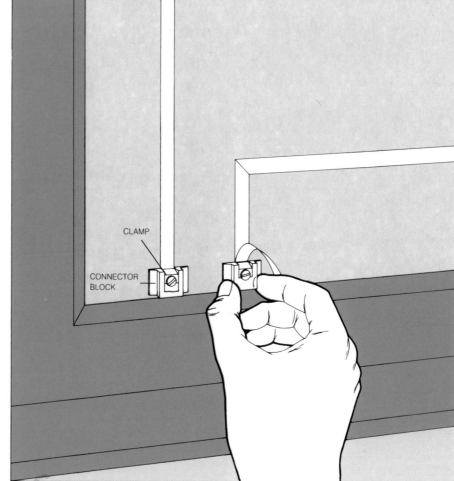

4 **Installing foil-connector blocks.** Pull one end of the foil away from the window edge and double it back so that a connector block will overlap the doubled-back foil by 3 mm. Stick the adhesive-backed block in place. Remove the screw and clamp from the block, pull the foil over the block and screw down the clamp over the foil; trim excess foil. Install a second block at the other end of the foil; connect circuit wires to the terminal screws on both blocks. Test the circuit.

Coat the tape with foil varnish, available from the foil supplier, to make it brittle and certain to break if the window does.

CLAMP

CONNECTOR BLOCK

An Electronic Vibration Detector

Installing the sensor. Remove the cover of the sensor and secure the unit to the frame of the door or window with the screws provided. Run a six-core cable from the control box to the sensor and, following the manufacturer's instructions, attach the wires to the terminal block. When installing more than one unit, wire the two power wires in parallel and the tamper and alarm wires in series, as described on pages 64–65. After connecting the wires, test the sensor by rapping on the door or window at the furthest point from the sensor. The light-emitting diode (LED) will light up if the sensor is activated; if the light does not come on, adjust the sensitivity control knob according to the manufacturer's instructions until the level is achieved. Screw on the sensor cover.

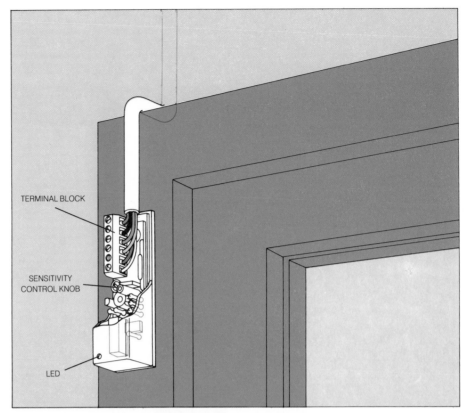

TERMINAL BLOCK

SENSITIVITY CONTROL KNOB

LED

Installing a Junction Box

Connecting the wires. If several sensors are installed in a room, connect them to a single cable from the control box by means of a junction box. Secure the back plate of the junction box to the wall or ceiling in an unobtrusive location. Connect the alarm and tamper wires in series and the power wires in parallel, as described on pages 64–65. In the junction box on the right, six-core cables from two inertia sensors are connected to a single cable leading back to the control box. The tamper circuit must always be connected to the anti-tamper terminals in the middle of the box.

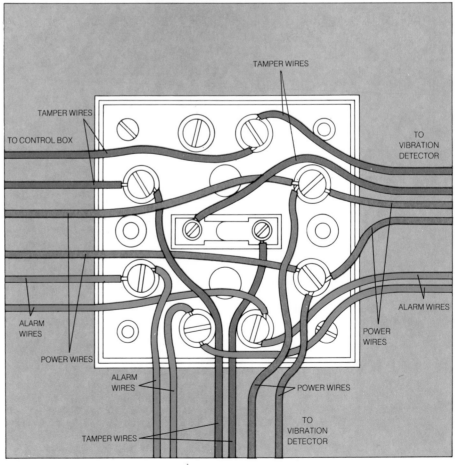

TAMPER WIRES

TAMPER WIRES

TO CONTROL BOX

TO VIBRATION DETECTOR

ALARM WIRES

ALARM WIRES

POWER WIRES

POWER WIRES

ALARM WIRES

POWER WIRES

TAMPER WIRES

TO VIBRATION DETECTOR

Detecting the Step of a Thief

1 **Laying a pressure mat.** Roll back the carpet and underlay and make sure that the exposed floor surface is clean, dry and even. Remove or punch in any protruding nail heads. Secure the pressure mat in position with drawing pins at the corner edges if the floor is timber *(right)* or with adhesive tape if the floor is concrete.

2 **Soldering the connections.** When more than one pressure mat is being installed, the sensor wires must be connected in parallel *(page 64)*; if the pressure mats are also fitted with tamper wires, these must be connected in series *(page 65)*. To connect each wire to its corresponding wire in the cable from the control box, first strip off 15 mm of insulation and twist the wires together tightly. While a helper supports the exposed wires in a convenient position, heat the wires with a soldering iron and touch resin-cored solder to the wires so that it runs over the joint. When the solder has cooled, insulate the connection with adhesive PVC tape, keeping the joint as flat as possible.

Insulate the bare ends of any spare wires on the last mat in a series with PVC insulating tape. Before relaying the carpet and underlay, secure the pressure mat wires and the cable to the floor with insulated staples or tape.

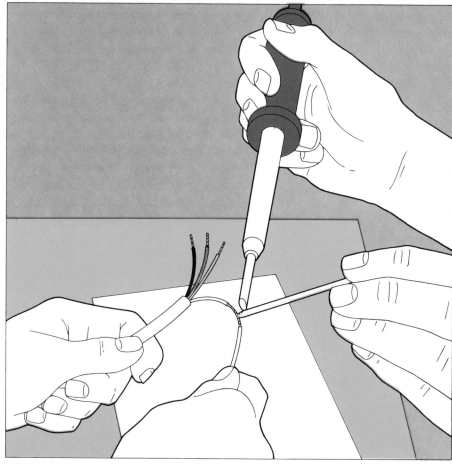

An Infra-Red Eye to Watch a Room

Positioning the sensor. A typical PIR detector is responsive to infra-red energy within a number of long-range zones and a smaller number of short-range zones; the maximum coverage is usually about 12 metres. It is designed to be installed at a height of roughly 2 metres, and should be sited in a corner rather than along a wall to gain the maximum benefit from its field of surveillance. To avoid false alarms, ensure that the detector is not aimed directly at windows, radiators, hot-air grilles or other points in a room where sudden temperature changes might trigger the sensor. Most PIR detectors are more sensitive to movement across their field of surveillance than to movement towards the sensor.

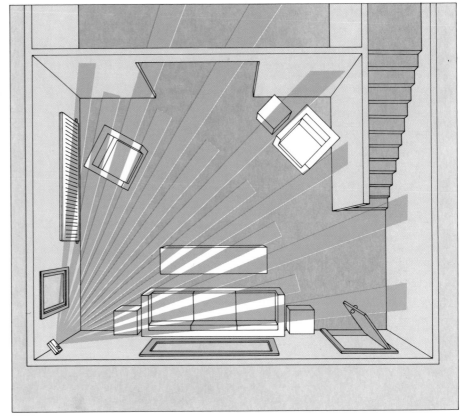

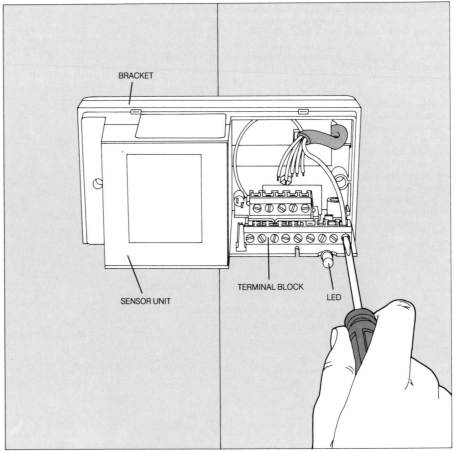

BRACKET

SENSOR UNIT

TERMINAL BLOCK

LED

Wiring the sensor. Hold the sensor bracket in position at the height recommended by the manufacturer and mark the positions of the screw holes on the wall. Remove the bracket and drill and plug the holes. Route a six or eight-core cable from the control box to the location of the sensor, thread the cable through the bracket and secure the bracket to the wall with the screws provided. Thread the cable through the back of the sensor unit and screw the unit to the bracket. Following the manufacturer's instructions, attach the cable wires to their appropriate terminals. Clip the protective cover on to the sensor unit. Test the detector by walking across the room—the light-emitting diode (LED) will light up when you enter the sensor's field of surveillance. If necessary, adjust the position of the sensor on the wall to gain maximum coverage; some models can be tilted upwards or downwards by inserting a strip of self-adhesive foam rubber between the bracket and the sensor unit.

A Panic Button for Emergencies

1 **Installing a flush mounting box.** Hold the box against the wall and pencil round its outline, then chip out a recess for the box with a cold chisel and hammer. Channel two-core cable—or, if a tamper circuit is used, four-core cable—from the control box to the panic button location. Punch out one of the knock-out holes in the mounting box, fit a rubber grommet to protect the cable, then insert the mounting box in the recess and thread the cable through the hole *(right)*. Mark the screw holes at the back of the box; drill and plug the holes, then screw the box to the wall. Make good the plaster round the mounting box.

On a timber-frame wall, cut a hole through the plasterboard with a trimming knife for the mounting box and attach clip-on flanges to the sides of the box. Thread a piece of string through the holes in the back of the box, then pull the string taut while positioning the face plate, to prevent the box falling through the hole. When the string is removed and the face plate screws are tightened, the flanges will be pulled against the inside face of the plasterboard.

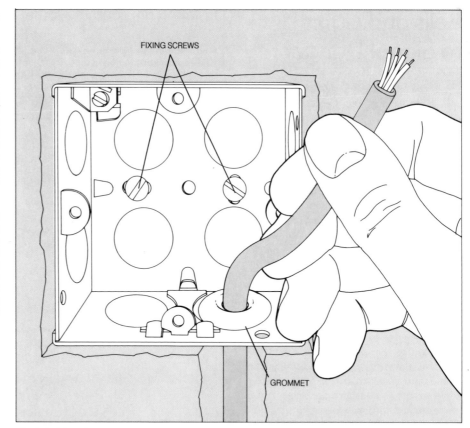

FIXING SCREWS

GROMMET

2 **Connecting the panic button.** Strip the ends of the cable wires and secure them to the terminals on the back of the panic button unit, following the manufacturer's instructions. Carefully fold the wires into the mounting box so that they do not get damaged, and secure the panic button face plate to the box with the screws supplied. Test the sensor by pressing the button; to release the button, insert and turn the key in the face plate.

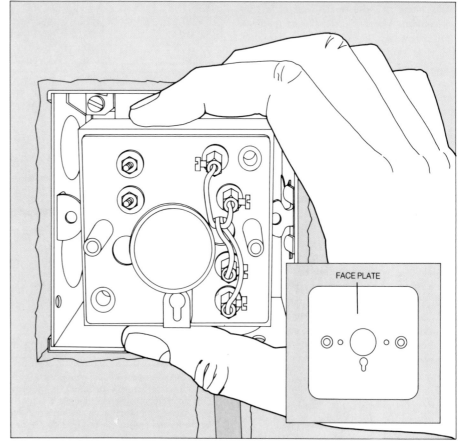

FACE PLATE

Bells and Lights to Signal Danger

The alarm in an alarm system may be a bell, siren or flashing light. Before you choose a particular type of alarm, seek the advice of the local police. Most authorities recommend audible alarms both outside and inside a house; the internal sounder deters the intruder if he manages to get in, and also alerts the occupants to his presence, while the outside sounder warns neighbours and passers-by that a break-in has taken place. An internal sounder is especially recommended for double-glazed houses, in which the external alarm may be difficult to hear.

Internal alarms should be mounted in a hallway or similar central position from which they can be heard by anyone in the house; they are wired to the positive hold-off supply to the external alarm and the negative alarm drive, as indicated in the manufacturer's instructions. Most exterior devices come in weathertight boxes (*right, above*); mount the box where a burglar cannot easily reach it—for example, under the eaves—and as close to the control box as convenient. Use an extension drill bit to drill a hole for the cable directly through the wall and into the box. For additional security you can install a self-activating alarm fitted with an anti-tamper device, which will sound if the wires are cut or the siren is interfered with.

The basic alarms depend on sound, but a flashing light outside can help police identify a house where an alarm is sounding. For this purpose a strobe—similar to those used for flash photography—is mounted on the alarm box, where it can be seen from the street, and wired to flash when the alarm sounds—and in some cases even when the alarm has stopped.

To wire strobe lights and other signalling devices, you simply link their wires to wires leading from the control panel, using terminal blocks (*right, below*). Strobes and most sirens must be wired according to positive and negative polarity; ensure that you keep to your colour-coding system in order to avoid faults.

Installing an External Alarm

1 Attaching a strobe light to the box. Using the strobe housing as a template, mark locations for bolt holes on the alarm casing, then drill the mounting holes and an extra hole to take the wiring. Fit a grommet into the wiring hole, then feed the strobe light wires through the hole and attach the strobe to the casing with the bolts provided. Tighten the nuts with a spanner. If necessary, unscrew the alarm unit from the casing to allow room for tightening the nuts.

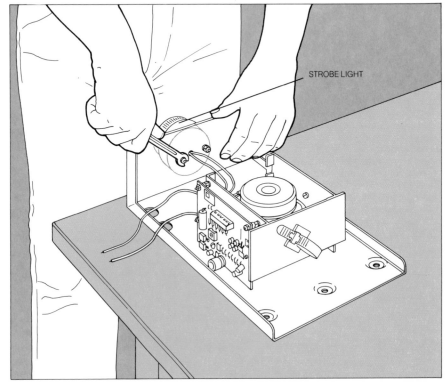

STROBE LIGHT

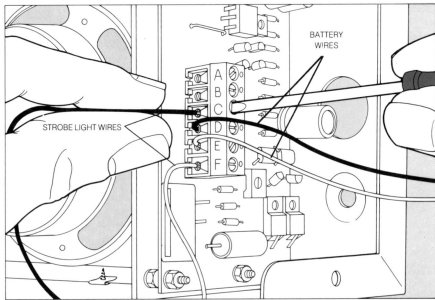

BATTERY WIRES

STROBE LIGHT WIRES

2 Linking the strobe and the alarm. Attach the wires from the strobe to terminals in the alarm unit according to the manufacturer's instructions supplied and screw on the battery holder for the alarm. Attach the battery to the box and prepare the battery wires for connection to the terminals, then insulate them with tape and tuck them away. Temporarily tape down the tamper switch until you are ready to put the system into operation.

3 Mounting the box. Run a length of four-core cable from the control box to the point on the inside wall that corresponds to the planned position of the alarm outside. Using an extension drill bit, drill a 6 mm hole through the outside wall. Hold the alarm casing against the outside of the wall, aligning the hole in the back of the casing with the hole in the wall, then drill and plug fixing positions in the brickwork and screw the alarm to the wall *(below)*. Push the four-core cable through the hole from the inside, and attach it to the alarm terminals according to the manufacturer's instructions supplied.

When all the components in the alarm system have been installed and tested *(page 72)*, connect the battery wires to the battery terminals; release the tamper switch and secure the alarm cover. Check that the alarm system is working by setting off a sensor. To check that the alarm is self-activating, disconnect the system from the mains and disconnect the control unit battery; the external alarm battery should then take over, and cause the alarm to sound until the control unit battery is reconnected.

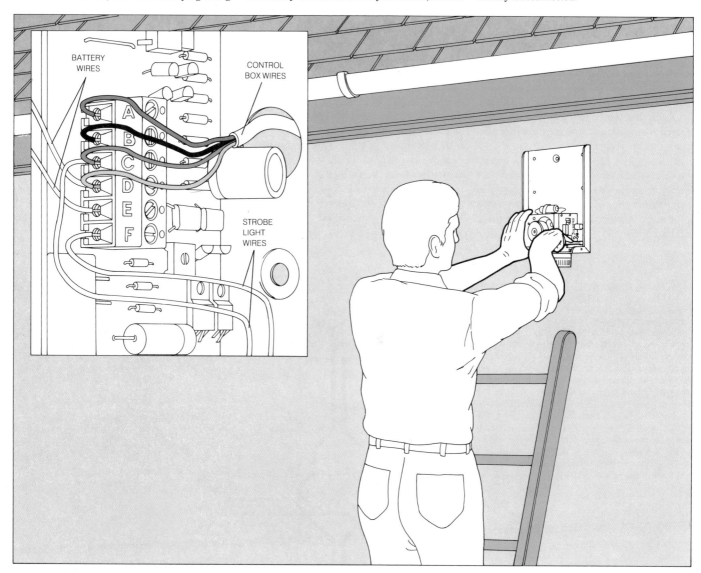

A Telephone Dialler for Peace of Mind—at a Price

An automatic telephone dialler, which sends out a pre-recorded alarm message to selected neighbours and friends, is an effective weapon against a burglar who disables conventional signalling devices. A dialler may be essential in a house located so far from neighbours that a conventional alarm cannot be seen or heard.

Diallers are expensive, but they are also ingenious and versatile. Some can be programmed to call several different numbers with different messages; others repeat a message for a certain period of time. Several models can monitor the condition of the phone lines, sounding an alarm if they are cut, and one model has a "line-seizing" feature that enables the device to override incoming calls.

Digital communicators send signals, as opposed to verbal messages, to a central monitoring station. Some monitoring stations can check on the units for a status report without disturbing the occupants if all is in order.

Controls and Switches to Bypass Sensors

Directly or indirectly, every component of a comprehensive alarm system is wired to the control box, which powers the system, receives signals from sensors, sends signals to alarms, and switches all or part of the system on and off. Some professionally installed systems incorporate separate remote control stations at which the system can be armed or disarmed, made operative or inoperative. For convenience, however, you may also wish to install individual control switches that allow you to enter a protected room without having to switch off a sensor at the control box.

The simplest type of control is a bypass switch *(below)* which, in the "off" position, disconnects one or more components to permit you to open a door or window protected by a magnetic sensor, for example, without affecting the rest of the system. Choose a bypass switch that is housed in a tough box and which is tamper-proof, with a red light to warn that the sensor is disarmed. The switches are wired with six-core cable, and should have the facility of connecting to either closed or open circuits.

Bypass switches are operated by either a key or a key pad, in which the user punches in a code of digits. The latter type may offer the facility to momentarily bypass a door sensor before reverting to its armed state; in this case, two key pads must be fixed on opposite sides of the door.

A less obtrusive control switch for doors is a bypass or shunt lock. This incorporates a switch so that when locked, the sensor is armed, but when unlocked, the sensor is bypassed. A shunt lock is wired to the sensor via a pre-assembled flexible loop, which allows the door to open and close without breaking the cable *(opposite page, above)*. To conceal the cable that runs between the shunt lock mortise and the cable loop, you can rout a channel across the inside face of the door; tack the cable in place, then fill in the channel with wood filler.

Working on the same principle is the shunt keep, where the bypass switch is housed in a box-type strike plate rather than in the lock itself. Shunt keeps are wired through the back of the doorframe *(opposite page, below)*; although they offer marginally less security, they are often preferred to shunt locks because the cable does not have to be routed across the door.

Both shunt locks and keeps are wired up using four-core cable. They can be used to bypass the sensor switch on the front or main exit door if the alarm system is not fitted with an entry-exit timer.

A Key-Operated Bypass Switch

Bypassing a magnetic door sensor. Install an eight-way junction box at the side of the architrave on a level with the sensor and connect the two with four-core cable. Drill and plug holes for the bypass switch in a convenient position close to the door handle and screw the back of the unit to the wall. Run a length of six-core cable from the terminals on the switch cover to the junction box, and another length from the junction box to the control unit; ensure that the tamper circuit is connected to the anti-tamper terminals in the middle of the junction box *(inset)*. When all connections have been made, secure the bypass switch cover to the back of the unit with the screws provided.

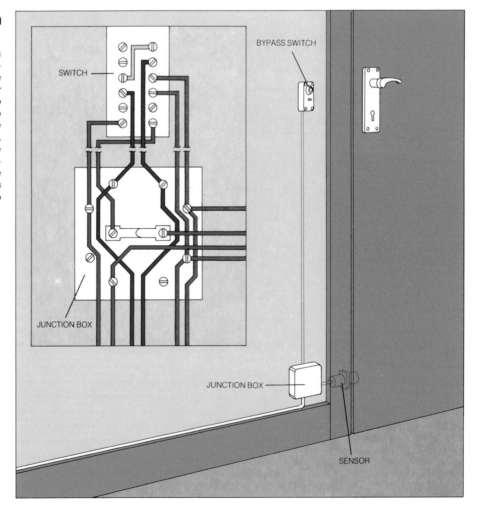

SWITCH

BYPASS SWITCH

JUNCTION BOX

JUNCTION BOX

SENSOR

A Shunt Mortise Lock

1 Installing the lock. Use a continuity tester to ascertain which are the shunt lock tamper wires and which the switch wires *(page 72)*. Use a drill and chisel to prepare a mortise for the lock in the door *(page 30)*, making the hole at least 15 mm deeper than the lock to allow for the wires. From the inside face of the door, drill a 6 mm hole into the back of the mortise. Ease the lock with its pre-attached cable into the mortise and pull the cable through the hole *(below)*. Leave about 150 mm of slack cable at the back of the mortise to allow for inspections. Tack the cable across the door to within 75 mm of the hinge side, using insulated staples.

2 Fitting the door loop. Screw the back of one of the loop boxes to the hinge side of the door and connect the shunt lock cable to its terminals. Attach the box cover with the screw provided. Secure the second loop box to the doorjamb at the same height as the first. Run a length of four-core cable from the sensor round the top of the doorframe and attach it to the terminals in the second loop box *(below)*. Screw on the second box cover. To test the installation, switch on the sensor circuit at the control box and lock the door; when you unlock the door, you should be able to open the door without tripping the sensor.

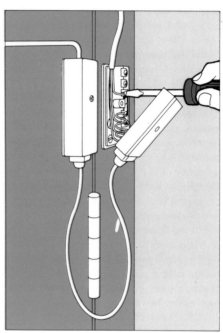

A Shunt Keep in the Jamb

Installing the keep. Fit a standard mortise lock in the door *(pages 30–31)*. Cut a mortise in the jamb for the shunt keep and a recess for its face plate. Drill a 6 mm hole through the architrave into the bottom of the mortise in the jamb. Run a four-core cable from the door sensor and lead it through the architrave into the mortise. Use a continuity tester to determine which are the sensor wires; connect the cable sensor wires to the shunt keep sensor wires by twisting and soldering, and connect the tamper wires in the same way. Seal the soldered joints with insulating tape. Insert the shunt keep carefully into the mortise; tuck the connected cables behind it, and secure it in the jamb with screws through the face plate.

Wiring the Control Box

You can gauge the capacity and sophistication of most control boxes by simply counting the terminals inside. The D.I.Y. box shown on these pages contains terminals serving closed circuits for door and window sensors, open circuits for pressure mats, vibration and passive infra-red detectors, the external alarm, and the batteries and recharger. More sophisticated boxes allow for the installation of additional components. Buy a control box with sufficient terminals to take any circuits you may wish to add in the future.

Power is supplied by either dry-cell or rechargeable batteries. Dry-cell batteries require changing periodically and should be tested weekly to make sure they are not running low; most control panels will have a facility to allow this. If you are using rechargeable batteries the charger should be connected to the mains supply by a qualified electrician.

Wiring the control box involves a maze of wires and cables, but requires patience rather than special skill. Observe your colour-coding system for differentiating between tamper, sensor and power wires, and remember to tag each cable with a coloured tape to identify separate sensor runs before connecting them to the control box. The procedure is the same for all boxes, although terminal arrangements vary from model to model; follow the manufacturer's instructions carefully, and seek professional help if in doubt.

1 **Wiring the connector strips.** Thread the cables from the sensors through one of the holes in the bottom of the control box, and strip 100 mm of the cable sheathing to expose the wires. Attach the two wires from each tamper circuit to pairs of adjacent terminals on one side of a connector strip. On the unwired side of the block, connect adjacent terminals with jumper wires so that one wire from each circuit is linked to one wire on the next as shown below on the left. To each free terminal at the end of the series of jumper wires, attach a wire which is long enough to reach to the terminal block in the control box (below, right). Then attach the sensor wires from each closed-circuit sensor to a second connector strip in the same way.

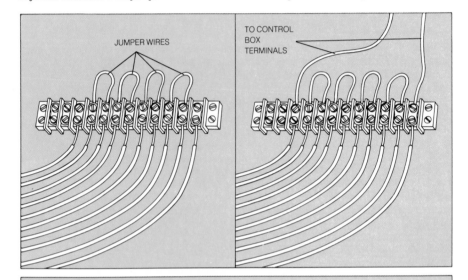

JUMPER WIRES

TO CONTROL BOX TERMINALS

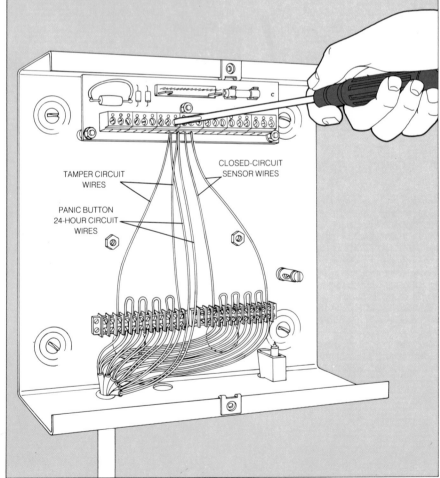

TAMPER CIRCUIT WIRES

CLOSED-CIRCUIT SENSOR WIRES

PANIC BUTTON 24-HOUR CIRCUIT WIRES

2 **Wiring the circuits.** Following the manufacturer's instructions, connect the wires from the tamper circuit and sensor circuit connector strips to their respective terminals in the control box. Depending on the design of your control box, connect the 24-hour circuit wires from the panic button to the tamper circuit terminals (right) or to their own separate terminals.

3 **Connecting the external alarm.** Route the cable from the external alarm into the control box and connect the positive and negative wires, tamper wires and alarm drive wire to their designated terminals. For the internal alarm wires, follow the manufacturer's instructions: these will either have their own designated terminals, or should be connected in parallel to the positive external alarm terminal and the negative terminal for the alarm drive circuit.

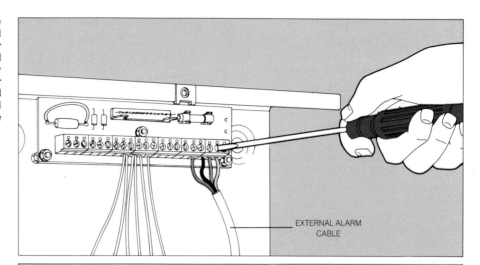

EXTERNAL ALARM
CABLE

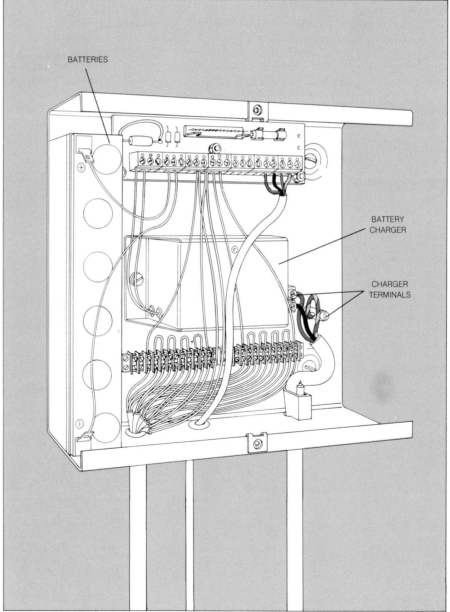

BATTERIES

BATTERY
CHARGER

CHARGER
TERMINALS

4 **Hooking up power.** Insert the batteries in the control box and connect their wires to their designated terminals. To test the system, attach the control box cover, then walk round the house tripping the sensors while a helper stands by at the control box to switch off and reset the alarm. After testing, remove the cover and attach the battery charger wires to their designated terminals. Feed a length of 0.5 mm three-core cable through the bottom of the control box and connect its wires to the charger terminals. Connect the alarm battery. Replace the cover, tucking the connector strips carefully inside the box. Get a qualified electrician to connect the battery charger cable to the mains via an unswitched spur with a 2 amp fuse.

Protecting Your Car and its Contents

After your house, your car is probably your most valuable possession. Common-sense precautions against theft include locking all doors and closing windows when leaving the car, even when garaged, and locking valuables out of sight in the boot. To guard against any but the most casual thief, however, some form of anti-theft device—in addition to a built-in steering lock—is essential.

The most important aspect of car security is deterrence: if the vehicle is obviously protected, an opportunist thief will usually let it alone. Locks that are clearly visible from outside the car include a locking hook linking the steering wheel and brake pedal and a combination lock on the handbrake. Special wheel nuts are available to prevent your wheels being stolen, and lockable petrol caps to stop your petrol being siphoned can be bought at motor accessory shops. Using an acid etching kit, you can etch the car's registration number on all the windows. Whatever security device

you choose, and even if you choose none, put a sticker on one of the windows advertising that the car is protected.

More sophisticated security is available in the form of alarms. These may either sound the car horn or have an independent siren; some come with a flashing light facility, and most systems immobilize the ignition when the alarm is triggered. Check the vehicle's instruction manual before installing an alarm with a switch that cuts off the ignition when you leave the car, as this could damage the transistorized circuits of cars with electronic ignition.

All alarm systems are powered by the car battery, and some models have stand-by batteries in case the main one is disconnected. The systems are armed in a number of different ways, the simplest being a key switch located either inside or outside the car. Some come on when the ignition is switched off, and must then be disarmed before the car can be driven again. Most systems have an alarm delay

facility which allows the owner to enter the car and switch off the system. The most sophisticated models can be operated from a distance by remote control.

A simple alarm system is triggered by contact switches on the doors. Vibration detectors react to the high-frequency vibrations of a forced entry; these alarms require professional installation. A more recent development is the ultrasonic alarm (below), which fills the car with sound waves and is triggered by any disturbance of the pattern of the air.

When installing an alarm, disconnect the battery leads before wiring up to avoid the possibility of a short-circuit. After installation, reconnect the battery and test the sensitivity of the alarm by rocking the car and rapping on the doors and windows; alarms that can be set off by an accidental jolt are more of a nuisance than a security measure. Adjust the sensitivity control knob as necessary to reduce the chances of a false alarm.

Installing an Ultrasonic Alarm

1 **Securing the sensor.** Using the mounting bracket as a template, mark and drill two holes for the fixing screws on the dashboard or at the rear of the car. Secure the bracket with the screws provided, then attach the sensor between the bracket arms and fasten it at the desired angle by tightening the screws in the arms (right). If the car has cloth-covered seats, the sensor must be fixed at a steep angle to overcome the acoustic absorption of the upholstery.

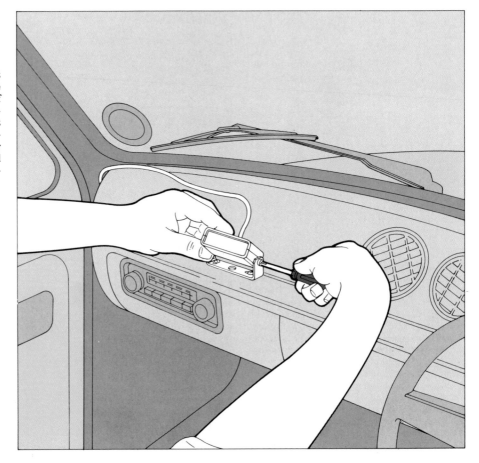

2 **Fitting the contact switches.** Open the car bonnet and drill a 14 mm hole for the switch close to the bonnet hinges or along the sill—the switch must be positioned so that it is depressed by the bonnet lid when closed but will spring upwards when the bonnet is opened. Do not locate the switch in a water gutter. Using the mounting plate as a template, drill two holes for the fixing screws. Slide the switch through its hole, slip on the mounting plate and secure the unit with the screws provided *(inset)*. If required, fit a second contact switch inside the car boot in the same way.

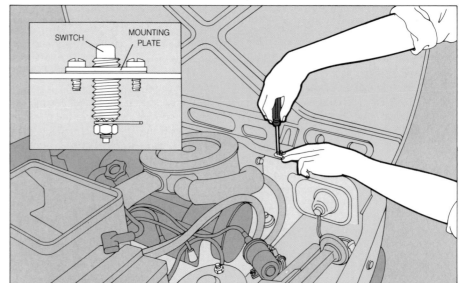

3 **Attaching the control box.** Secure the control box in a protected position in the engine compartment, using the self-tapping screws provided *(right)*. Prepare routes for the cables by drilling a hole through the bulkhead from the car interior into the engine compartment and, if a contact switch is fitted in the boot, from the car interior into the boot. Fit grommets into the holes to protect the cables from the metal edges.

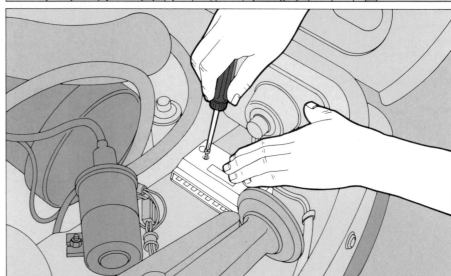

4 **Connecting the system.** Slot the on-off switch into its mounting bracket, screw on the flange to secure the switch, and secure the bracket in an accessible location close to the driving seat with the screws provided *(right)*. Following the manufacturer's instructions, run the power supply from the car battery to the on-off switch and from there to the control box. Connect the contact switches and the sensor to the appropriate terminals on the control box with the cables provided. Connect the earth terminal on the control box to a convenient point on the chassis. To sound the alarm, the control box may be connected either to the car horn or to an independent siren. The alarm delay facility and the sensitivity of the ultrasonic sensor can be adjusted by removing the dust covers on the control box and turning the appropriate knobs.

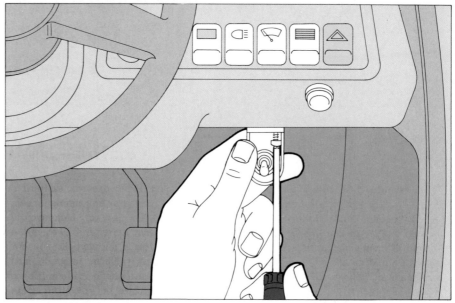

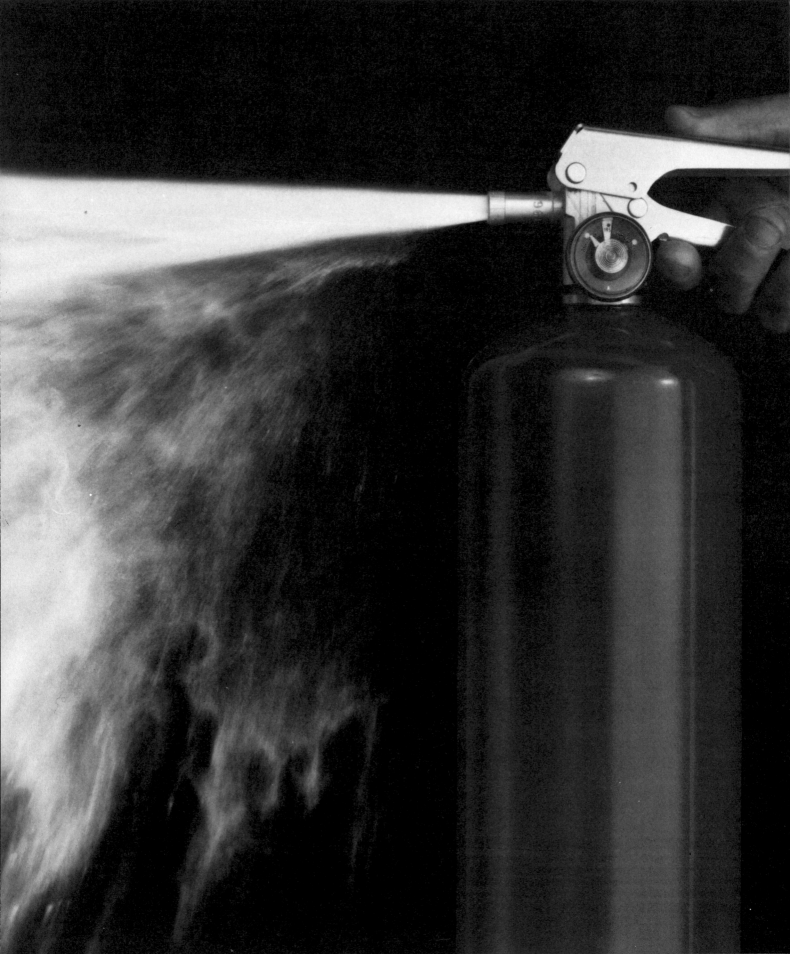

3

Defences Against Fire

A burst of fire-taming dust. When the handle of a dry chemical fire extinguisher is squeezed, a stream of dust squirts towards the fire. Aimed at the base of the flames, the powder forms a blanket that smothers the blaze. Dry chemical extinguishers are effective on most kinds of fire, but other types of extinguisher *(pages 97–98)* have specialized uses.

Building and wiring regulations specify standards for home construction that make houses relatively fireproof. For example, regulations in the United Kingdom require walls and floors between a house and an attached garage to be constructed of fire-resistant materials, and any door connecting the two must be able to resist fire for at least half an hour. Similarly, all external and load-bearing walls must be built of non-combustible materials.

Many older houses, however, were not built in accordance with these requirements, and even today's regulations do not require builders to avoid every hazardous design or to incorporate all the safety features that can reduce the probability of fire, inhibit its spread once it starts, and make the house easier to escape from. A master bedroom situated away from children's bedrooms, for example, offers a peaceful retreat for parents but may make it impossible for them to reach the children in the event of a fire. Bedroom windows that are set high above the floor offer desirable privacy—but no child and few adults would be able to escape a fire through them.

Lower windows are not easy to install, but many other hazards built into an existing home can be remedied fairly simply. Nailing fire-resistant plasterboard to timber-frame walls *(pages 93–94)* is an elementary job; flame-retardant hardboard can be nailed over timber floorboards *(page 92)* and inflammable furnishings can be specially treated *(pages 90–91)*. If the door at the top of a cellar stairway is the old-fashioned panelled type or the modern, inexpensive hollow-core flush type, replace it with a solid-core flush door, which retards the spread of flames much better than the others. If there is no door to close off cellar stairs, install one. Standard doors connecting the living area of a house to an attached garage and at other strategic openings should be replaced with fire doors or adapted to make them fire-resistant *(page 95)*. And common-sense safeguards, such as the small extinguisher shown on the opposite page and smoke detectors *(page 61)*, should be added to ordinary household equipment.

Most fires are caused by carelessness and ignorance. Overloading electrical sockets, frying foods at too high a temperature and leaving the television on overnight are all examples of the kind of easily made mistake that can lead to a conflagration, and no amount of safety devices can provide infallible protection. Knowing how to avoid a fire is the first step in safeguarding yourself and your family *(page 90)*. Knowing what to do if a fire breaks out is the next step. Ensure that every member of your household is acquainted with the advice on page 100, so that in the event of an emergency they will be able to escape from a fire with the minimum confusion and risk of injury.

Easy Ways to Make Your House Hard to Burn

Each year about 800 people in the U.K. die in home fires, and many times that number are injured. Much of this tragic loss could be avoided by common-sense living habits and simple alterations in house structures and furnishings.

Fire hazards concentrate in certain parts of the house—not necessarily in the way you might expect. Kitchen fires, fuelled by fat in overheated pans or inside extractor fans, are the most common type of household fire. Numerous as they are, such blazes account for only 5 per cent of fire fatalities, because someone is usually present to extinguish the flames.

Fires in living rooms, although they amount to only 10 per cent of all house fires, account for 48 per cent of the fatalities. Most are caused by smokers who fall asleep, allowing glowing embers to drop on to sofa and chair cushions. Ignorance causes other fires. The heat from the electronic innards of television sets, for instance, has started fires when sets were left on overnight or operated on a carpeted floor: the carpet pile can block cooling vents under the set.

Fires like this can usually be prevented by following the instructions that come with appliances and by observing the safety rules drilled into everyone from childhood. But not even the most vigilant can guard against fires started by lightning bolts, exploding gas mains or, in some regions, forest fires.

Although you cannot guarantee that a fire will not start, you can make it harder for the flames and fumes to spread. Begin by taking stock of your home furnishings. Carpets made with man-made fibres, and the covering and filling materials used for furniture nowadays, are highly inflammable and can give off toxic fumes when burning, limiting evacuation time to a matter of minutes. Recent legislation in the U.K. specifies flame-retardant treatment for textiles used in home furnishings, but older furnishing fabrics generally have not been treated.

Ready-made treatments suitable for D.I.Y. application are available, or you can add such protection yourself with fire-retardant solutions mixed from chemicals bought from chemical supply companies or chemists. The recipes in the chart (opposite page, below) are intended for materials containing cellulose: vegetable-fibre fabrics such as cotton, rayon or linen, alone or blended with synthetics; wallpaper, including the kind made with grass; and even Christmas trees. Pure synthetics such as nylon, and animal-fibre fabrics such as silk and wool, resist flame without treatment. The solutions are not harmful and will not discolour fabrics. They are meant to be used on furnishings, which are cleaned rarely if at all, since washing the fabric removes the protection.

But the furnishings of a house are not the only danger. Some building materials can spread fire rapidly from one room to another. Use the chart on the opposite page, above, to determine which materials are safest.

If a wall or ceiling is finished in an inflammable material—or, like some garage walls, not finished at all—the only good remedy is replacement with safer materials (pages 93–94). For extra protection you can use intumescent paint which reacts to the heat of a fire by puffing up into a layer of insulation. It is available for indoor or outdoor use and can be applied either by brush, roller or spraygun.

To prevent the upward passage of smoke and flames through floors, you can nail sheets of flame-retardant hardboard over the floorboards as shown on page 92. The sheets should be tightly joined and pushed right up to the edges of the room to prevent any smoke from getting through. If you have underfloor insulation between the joists, make sure that it is made of a non-combustible material.

Doors can also be made fire-resistant. Interior doors can easily be replaced with fire doors which come in standard sizes and are categorized according to the length of time they will hold back a fire. Alternatively, existing doors can be modified by the application of special fire-resistant boards (page 95). All fire doors should be fitted with automatic door closers to ensure they are not left open (page 95).

A fire that attacks from outside the house is more difficult to guard against. But in forest-fire country, there is a way to make a house less likely to burn. Simply clear easily ignited vegetation from the area around the house with a scythe and replace it with lawn and fire-resistant plants. The Forestry Commission or a reputable nursery will advise you on which species are suitable. In a protective green belt around the house, these plants can help to hold a forest fire at bay.

A Safety Check List

☐ Do not leave lighted cigarettes lying around where they might fall on to carpets or furniture. Do not smoke in bed.

☐ Switch off all gas or electric heaters before going to bed, and make sure that no cooking appliances are still on.

☐ Never extinguish cigarettes in a waste-paper bin. Always use an ashtray, and make sure there are no smouldering stubs when emptying it.

☐ Keep cigarette lighters and matches well out of the reach of children.

☐ Always place a guard in front of an unattended gas or open fire.

☐ Never use a match to look for a gas leak; use soapy water brushed round joints.

☐ Do not dry clothes in front of a fire.

☐ Keep your distance from an open fire if you are wearing loose garments.

☐ Do not use makeshift electrical connections, nor run flex under a carpet where it might become frayed and dangerous without being noticed.

☐ Keep flex away from hot surfaces such as cookers or fires.

☐ Unplug electrical appliances when not in use. Never plug appliances into a light socket instead of a wall socket.

☐ When using a deep-fat frier, be sure not to overfill it or leave it unattended.

☐ Do not obstruct halls, stairways, or any other area that might be a means of escape in the event of fire.

☐ Secure the front door with a lock that can be opened from inside without a key. If windows have locks, use a common key for all of them, keeping it ready to hand.

☐ Fit door chains or bolts where they can be reached by children or people crawling under the smoke and heat of a fire.

Fire Ratings for Building Materials

Flame-Spread Rating	Wall or Ceiling Material
Class O	Masonry Glass Gypsum plaster Asbestos-free fibreboard Plasterboard
Class 1	Flame-retardant hardboard Flame-retardant plywood Vermiculite chipboard Flame-retardant fibreboard Pressure-treated timber Flame-retardant ceiling tiles
Class 2–3	Untreated chipboard Untreated hardboard Untreated plywood
Class 4	Untreated fibreboard Untreated wall panelling Low-density timber

Picking a safe material. Common coverings for walls and ceilings are grouped into five classes of flame-spread ratings. Tested in accordance with British Standards for fire propagation, ratings range from Class O, for wholly non-combustible materials, to Class 4. Classifications can be improved by flame-retardant treatment, and certain surface coverings such as plaster; conversely some paints will make the fire spread more rapidly. Class O and 1 materials are recommended for the walls of large rooms and spaces such as living rooms, halls, staircases and kitchens. For ceilings and the walls of smaller rooms, Class 3 is the minimum recommendation. Class 4 materials are not recommended. Manufacturers of building materials mark many of their products, including ceiling tiles and wall panelling, with flame-spread ratings.

Flame-Proofing Recipes

Material to be Treated	Recipe
Permanent-press fabrics (blends of vegetable and synthetic fibres)	340 grams diammonium phosphate 2.3 litres water
Untreated vegetable-fibre fabrics	200 grams borax 85 grams boric acid 2.3 litres water
Paper and cardboard	200 grams borax 85 grams boric acid 140 grams diammonium phosphate 1 teaspoon liquid dishwashing detergent 4 litres water
Christmas tree	3 litres sodium silicate (water glass) 2.3 litres water 2 teaspoons liquid dishwashing detergent

Mixing and applying the chemicals. The fire-retarding solutions in the chart are prepared by dissolving the ingredients in the quantity of hot tap water called for in the recipe.

To treat fabrics and paper products, wet them thoroughly with the appropriate solution by spraying or dipping, then allow them to dry flat. To treat a Christmas tree, spray or paint the tops and undersides of branches with the water-glass solution. Let the tree dry, then treat it again to ensure that each needle and branch is coated with a shiny, fire-retardant glaze.

Walls and Floors to Contain a Blaze

Nowadays, new houses in the U.K. generally contain built-in barriers to the spread of fire. In addition, all internal floors, walls and doors—especially those connecting the living area to an attached garage—must conform to the fire-resistance specifications of the U.K. building regulations. However, if you live in an older house—or if you are converting an old property or building a new extension—there are a number of measures you should take to ensure adequate protection.

Upgrading an existing structure usually involves the addition of a new layer of fire-resistant material, such as nailing flame-retardant hardboard sheets to a timber floor *(below)* to protect against smoke and flames spreading upwards through the house. In new construction, all stud walls should be built with gypsum plasterboard, which is naturally flame-resistant. Existing walls can be improved by adding a layer of plasterboard and staggering the joints; and the ceiling of an attached garage should be clad with plasterboard if a second storey is built over it.

For extra protection, use a slightly more expensive variety of plasterboard specifically designed for fire walls. Its gypsum core is combined with ground vermiculite and fibreglass; when the plasterboard is exposed to heat, the water in the vermiculite crystals is gradually released as steam, holding the fire back, while the fibreglass maintains the structural integrity of the plasterboard and prevents it from crumbling. Depending on the construction of the rest of the building, this will hold a fire at bay for almost an hour.

In the U.K., the special flame-resistant plasterboard sheets are 12 mm thick and generally measure 2440 by 1220 mm, although other sizes can be ordered. The sheets are usually installed vertically, like ordinary plasterboard, and the edges can be concealed with paper tape and premixed joint compound.

To prepare the walls, move the electrical switches and sockets outwards slightly, and nail strips of timber to the doorframe, so that both the jambs and the electrical fixtures will be flush with the face of the plasterboard. If any ducts or pipes run through the wall, frame them with 100 by 50 mm timber to provide nailing surfaces for the plasterboard *(page 94)*.

All strategic doorways, such as those connecting a house to an attached garage, or at the head of a staircase to an attic conversion, must be fitted with fire doors. There are two types of fire door—fire-check and fire-resisting—and they are categorized by their ability to withstand a fire in terms of stability and integrity. Their stability fails when the structure of the door collapses; their integrity is lost if there is a crack or opening through which flames or smoke can pass. A fire-resisting door has greater integrity than a fire-check door, usually due to intumescent strips, which swell up under heat to seal the gaps between the door and its frame.

Manufactured fire doors usually consist of a filling of plasterboard or mineral core encased in sheets of plywood or hardboard. Some have reinforced glass panels and the frames are made of pressure-treated wood.

If you do not wish to buy a new door, you can modify an existing one by cladding it with fire-resistant asbestos-free sheets and attaching intumescent strips around the edge of the door or its frame *(page 95)*. Fit an automatic door closer to ensure that the door remains closed at all times. The finished door should be at least 44 mm thick, with doorstops 25 mm deep.

Treating a Timber Floor

Securing flame-retardant hardboard sheets. Butt the first sheet tightly into one corner of the room, pushing it underneath the skirting boards if possible, and secure it to the timber floor with 25 mm hardboard or annular nails spaced 10 mm in from the edges and at intervals of about 200 mm. Butt the remaining sheets tightly against each other so that there are no gaps for smoke and flames to seep through, and secure them in the same way. Cut the sheets if necessary to ensure that the joints between them do not coincide with the joints between floorboards.

Putting Up
Gypsum Plasterboard

Putting up the sheets. Mark the centre of each stud on the ceiling and floor. Put a plasterboard sheet against the studs at one end of the wall and push the sheet tight against the ceiling with a foot-operated lever, such as a wedge-shaped piece of wood on a scrap of pipe. Align the edge of the sheet with the centre of a stud and drive several plasterboard nails through the plasterboard into the studs *(right)*. The final blow should set each nail just below the surface and make a gentle depression, or "dimple", around the nail head, without tearing the paper face of the plasterboard.

Working from the centre of the sheet outwards to the edges, drive pairs of nails into each stud every 300 mm, with the second nail in each pair 50 mm from the first. Drive single nails every 200 mm around the edges of the sheet, about 9 mm from the edge.

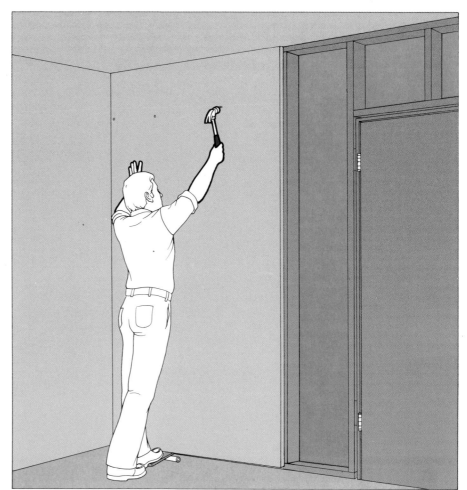

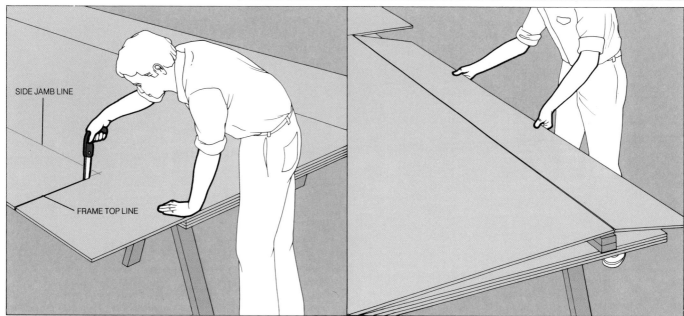

SIDE JAMB LINE

FRAME TOP LINE

Fitting plasterboard round a door. Measure from the ceiling to the top of the side jamb nearest the installed sheet of plasterboard, then measure from the edge of this sheet to the top and bottom of the jamb. Subtract 6 mm from each measure-ment, make matching measurements and marks in from the edges of a sheet of plasterboard, and draw lines connecting the marks. Cut along the shorter line with a compass saw *(above, left)*. Score the longer line with a trimming knife, prop the sheet behind the scored line with two long 100 by 50 mm timber boards and push down the edge of the sheet abruptly to snap the core *(above, right)*. Slice through the backing paper between the cut pieces and install the sheet.

Fitting around pipes and ducts. If a pipe runs through the wall, butt-nail a horizontal 100 by 50 mm board below the pipe to the stud on each side and nail a vertical 100 by 50 mm board next to the pipe between the horizontal 100 by 50 mm board and the head plate of the wall. Fasten the pipe to the vertical and horizontal boards with a metal pipe strap *(inset, right)*. For a duct, butt-nail horizontal 100 by 50 mm boards 18 mm above and below the duct, and nail vertical 100 by 50 mm boards 18 mm away from each side of the duct *(inset, far right)*.

Measure from the ceiling to the top and bottom of the pipe or duct and to the centre of the horizontal 100 by 50 mm boards; measure from the nearest sheet of plasterboard to the left and right edges of the pipe or duct and to the centre of the vertical 100 by 50 mm boards. Transfer all these measurements to a sheet of plasterboard, then outline the pipe or duct and the 100 by 50 mm boards. Cut a hole for the pipe or duct with a compass saw. Cut the plasterboard along the centres of the 100 by 50s, stopping level with the centre of the pipe or duct, then cut at right angles into the hole. Nail the larger piece to the wall *(right)*, then the smaller one.

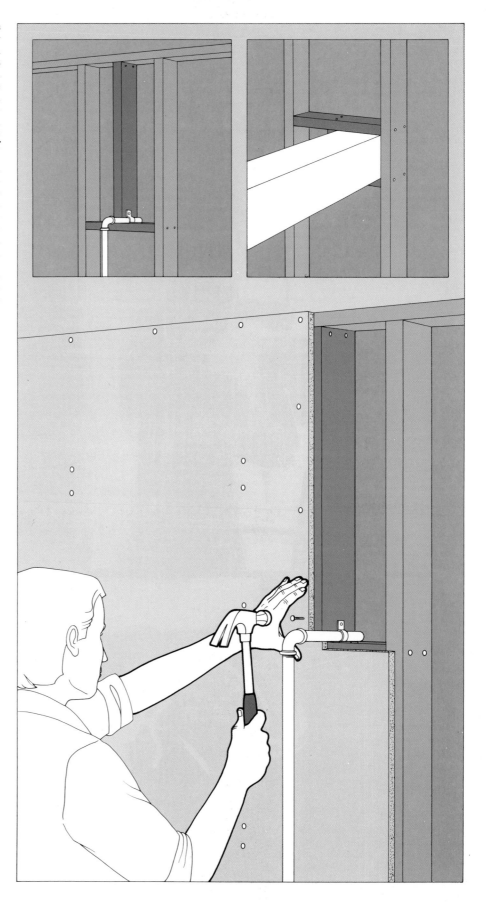

Making a Door Fire-Resistant

1 **Attaching the cladding.** Remove the door from its hinges, lay it on trestles or sawhorses and take off the door handle and any other protruding fittings. Mark out a sheet of 6 mm fire-resistant asbestos-free board to the same size as the door. Cover one entire face of the door with PVA glue, then lay the sheet in position and secure it with panel pins at intervals of 230 mm around the edge of the door. When the glue has dried—after about half an hour—turn the door over and drill a hole through the fire-resistant board for the spindle, using the existing hole in the door as a guide. Attach a second board to the exposed face of the door as before, then drill through from the other side for the spindle.

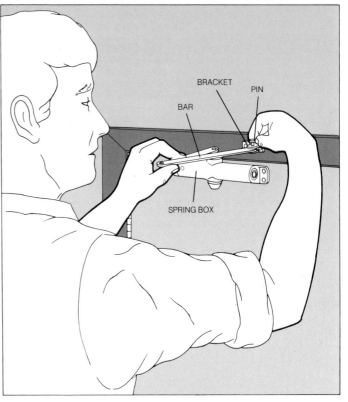

2 **Installing intumescent strips.** Using the techniques described on pages 33–34, rout a groove 10 mm wide and 2 mm deep along the top, bottom and side edges of the door. Cut intumescent strips to length with a trimming knife and secure them in the grooves with PVA glue, making sure they are flush with door edges and will not catch when the door is opened and closed. Rehang the door; if necessary, reposition the hinges and the doorstops on the frame to allow for the increased thickness of the door.

3 **Fitting the door closer.** Close the door, mark the position for the automatic door closer on the door and the top of the frame, using the template provided. Remove the cover of the spring box and secure the box in place with the screws provided. Screw the bracket for the bar to the doorframe. Connect the pivoted bar to the spring box with the screw provided and to the bracket with the bracket pin. Test the action of the door; if necessary, adjust the tension of the spring by turning the screw on the end of the spring box. Finally, replace the spring box cover.

Extra Safety from a Sprinkler System

A home sprinkler system, a less extensive version of the ones that protect factories, warehouses and office buildings, does more than retard fires: it puts them out. Installing a sprinkler system throughout an existing house is prohibitively expensive, but adding one to a basement workshop *(below)*, where serious fires often start, is a more feasible proposition.

Sprinklers are excellent protection because they work automatically. Mains-fed water pipes run through the ceiling joists of each storey. Sprinkler heads (plain *(inset)* or flush-mounted for concealment) are spaced along the pipes to serve as nozzles. They are turned on by the heat of a fire, each one dousing up to 46 square metres of floor area, depending on the angle of the sprinkler head and the height of the room.

In a fire, a fusible link in the sprinkler head melts, allowing two struts in the centre of the head to fall clear and release a plug. Water pours out, broken into a fine, even spray by a deflector at the bottom of the head.

In the basement installation below, the system is connected to the mains supply after the main stoptap. A backflow check valve keeps sprinkler water out of the domestic water pipes, and a flow sensor sounds an alarm if water moves through the sprinklers. A test valve simulates the discharge of a sprinkler head to test the alarm and measure the flow of water.

If you are building a new home, installation throughout the house is worth considering. The cost is roughly the same as wall-to-wall carpeting for all rooms—but the possible savings in the event of fire are significant.

As sprinkler systems use so much water, it is necessary to obtain a licence from the water authorities, who may insist on installing a meter.

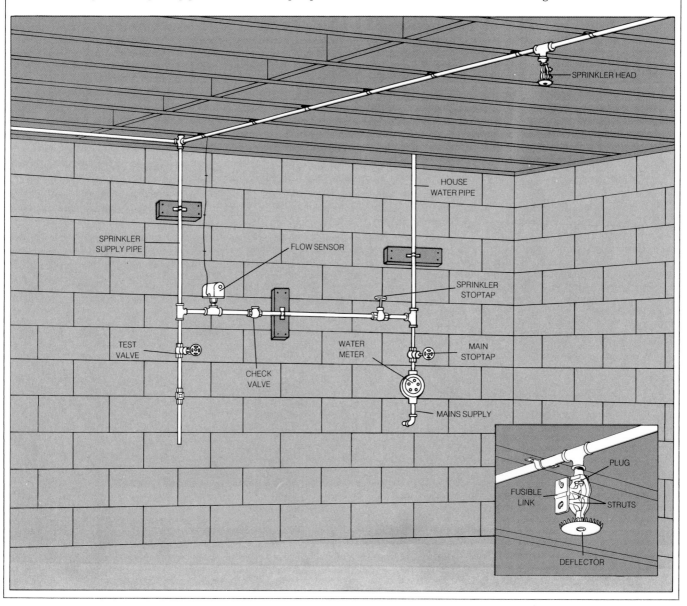

SPRINKLER HEAD

HOUSE WATER PIPE

SPRINKLER SUPPLY PIPE

FLOW SENSOR

SPRINKLER STOPTAP

TEST VALVE

WATER METER

MAIN STOPTAP

CHECK VALVE

MAINS SUPPLY

PLUG

FUSIBLE LINK

STRUTS

DEFLECTOR

Putting Out a Small Fire With a Hand Extinguisher

Nearly everyone has had an unsettling experience with fire or the threat of fire inside a house. Sometimes the experience, which may be a frantic search for a cigarette dropped behind a sofa cushion, or a carelessly held oven glove smouldering over a hob, is soon ended. Such fires, though potentially dangerous, are generally inconsequential, and easily smothered, brushed away or stamped out.

With a larger fire, such as paper burning in a wastepaper basket or a pan of fat on fire on the cooker, the same measures would be ineffective and dangerous. These fires are serious—yet in their early stages they are often contained in a small space and many can be easily extinguished if you react quickly. For example, flames in an oven can be put out by closing the door and turning off the heat. A fat fire in a pan or a deep-fat fryer can be extinguished with a fibreglass fire blanket lowered over the flames, or by covering the pan with a metal lid or large baking tin. Turn off the gas or electricity, keep the pan covered and do not attempt to move it. Never try to carry a pan of burning oil outside. Never use water to put out either a fat or an electrical fire; it may spread the flames. An electrical fire can often be stopped before it gets well started by pulling out the plug or turning off electricity at the consumer unit or fusebox. To fight an upholstery fire, on the other hand, water works best. Beat out the

flames with a damp towel or douse them with a pan of water. Then you can carry the cushion or piece of furniture out of doors and soak it thoroughly.

If your clothes catch fire, roll on the ground or floor to smother the flames. Never run. When someone else's clothes are on fire, force the victim to the ground and roll him over and over. Use a rug, blanket, coat, or fire blanket to help smother the flames, taking care not to obstruct the victim's breathing. When the fire is out, wrap the victim in a warm blanket and call an ambulance.

All of these small fires, with the single exception of burning clothes, can be put out much more safely with a portable fire extinguisher, which allows you to quench the flames from a distance.

Extinguishers come with a variety of fire-fighting agents, the commonest being dry chemical powder, ordinary water or carbon dioxide. Also available are foam, and vaporizing liquids. Each of these smothers a fire by depriving it of oxygen, and each is specifically designed for one or more types of fire. A Class A fire is fed by a solid fuel, such as wood or paper. A Class B fire involves a burning liquid such as fat or oil. And in the U.K. a Class C fire is one involving gas or a live electrical circuit; in Australia, Class C signifies a fire involving gas only, and Class E means an electrical fire. Use the chart on the opposite page to

select fire extinguishers for your home. For complete protection, you will need more than one: an extinguisher used against a class of fire for which it is not clearly labelled can actually increase the intensity of a fire. Learn how to operate each extinguisher you buy, and check all extinguishers once a month to see that they are fully charged.

Locate extinguishers around the house wherever there may be danger of fire, especially in the kitchen, garage, cellar and workshop. Mount them near exit doorways where they are visible and accessible, no more than 1.5 metres above the floor. Fire blankets should be near the cooker but not so close that you cannot get at them if the hot-plate turns into a ball of fire.

If a fire starts, alert others to evacuate the house and to call the fire brigade. Then, if the fire has not spread—and if it is not fed by plastics or foam rubber, which often produce poisonous fumes—use a fire extinguisher to douse the flames by the method shown on page 98. If the fire continues to burn after the extinguisher is empty, leave the room, close the door behind you and wait outside for the firemen. Always vacate the room after using carbon dioxide or vaporizing liquids in a small enclosed area; their toxic and asphyxiating qualities are such that you may be overwhelmed if you stay behind, even after the fire has been doused.

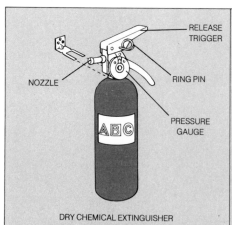

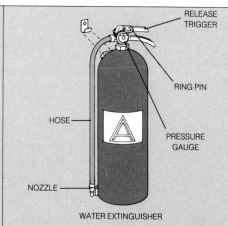

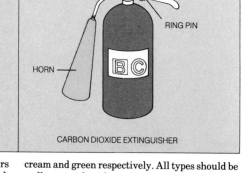

An arsenal of extinguishers. Fire extinguishers of different types can be identified by their appearance and, in the U.K., by their distinguishing colour. Multipurpose dry chemical models *(above, left)* have a nozzle or hose, with a blue label or sometimes a blue container; water extinguishers *(above, centre)* have a flexible hose and are red; and carbon dioxide units *(above, right)* discharge through a horn and have a black label or body. Foam and vaporizing liquid devices are coloured cream and green respectively. All types should be wall-mounted, with a safety pin that immobilizes the operating lever to prevent an accidental discharge. The best devices have an indicator to show whether they have been used or not.

The Right Type for Every Blaze

Type of Extinguisher	Class of Fire	Capacity	Weight	Range of Stream	Discharge Time	Advantages	Limitations
Multipurpose (dry chemical)	A, B or C	3 kg 6 kg 9 kg	5.4 kg 9.6 kg 15.4 kg	4 m 5 m 6 m	6 sec 10 sec 18 sec	Puts out all classes of fire; light-weight; inexpensive	May not completely extinguish a deep-seated upholstery fire; leaves residue
Stored pressure (water)	A	6 kg 9 kg	9.8 kg 11.9 kg	6 m 8 m	50 sec 70 sec	Longer discharge time; greater range	Must be protected from freezing; initial discharge might create more smoke, making visibility difficult
Carbon dioxide	B or C	2 kg 5 kg	5.1 kg 11.7 kg	3 m 5 m	14 sec 24 sec	Leaves no residue	Dissipates in wind; carbon dioxide "snow" may burn skin; eliminates oxygen around immediate area

Selecting an extinguisher. The main purpose of this chart is to help you balance the advantages and limitations of various fire extinguishers. Multipurpose dry chemical models, which are intended for all kinds of fire, make it unnecessary to classify a fire before extinguishing it. Though lighter and cheaper than other kinds, they do not work as well against Class A fires as water, and leave behind a powder that is difficult to clean up. A water extinguisher, though limited in application, lets you fight a fire longer and at a safer distance than other types. Carbon dioxide extinguishers, more costly than dry chemical or water models, leave no residue after a Class B or C fire. All extinguishers bought in the U.K. should conform to BS 5423, carry the Fire Offices' Committee label of approval and should be at least the size of the smallest units in the chart. Larger units expel their contents at a faster rate, but they are heavy and offer little improvement in range or discharge time.

How to Use an Extinguisher

Operating a fire extinguisher. Pull the ring pin from the extinguisher to free the release trigger, stand at least 1.5 metres from the fire and discharge the extinguisher at the base of the flames by squeezing the release trigger. If the stream from the extinguisher splatters burning material, back away from the fire, then play the stream on the fire, sweeping slowly from side to side, until you have emptied the extinguisher.

Safe Exits From an Upstairs Window

The safest means of escape from an upper room in case of emergency is a ladder or stairway secured to the external wall. Besides being expensive to install, however, such a permanent fixture offers easy access to intruders, and an exit route that can be stored inside the house when not in use is more suitable for most private houses.

A flexible ladder that unfolds in sections is a good alternative to a fixed ladder or steps. Most ladders come in 3 metre lengths to run from a first floor window. Extensions for the ladder can be added for higher windows, and the supporting brackets can be secured either outside the window—as shown on the right—or, with their openings facing down, on the inside of the wall. A second means of escape is provided by a sling running through a braking unit (below); cradles can be fitted in place of the slings for the use of children.

Descending from a window by either ladder or sling requires considerable agility and level-headedness; elderly people especially must take great care when using them. It is also essential to check regularly that they are firmly secured. Seek professional advice if you are in doubt about which fixings to use, and have the braking unit on a sling descent checked and serviced by the manufacturer.

An emergency steel ladder. Using the template provided, mark fixing holes for the brackets on the external wall just below the window. Drill and plug the holes for the stainless steel screws supplied, and secure the brackets with their openings facing upwards. To prepare the ladder for use, slot the top rung into the bracket openings and let the ladder drop down the wall; as the hinged sections unfold, spacers will automatically project against the wall to allow a user to gain a firm foothold on each step. After installation and at regular intervals, test the security of the fixings by attaching the ladder and weighting it with two people standing on the bottom rung.

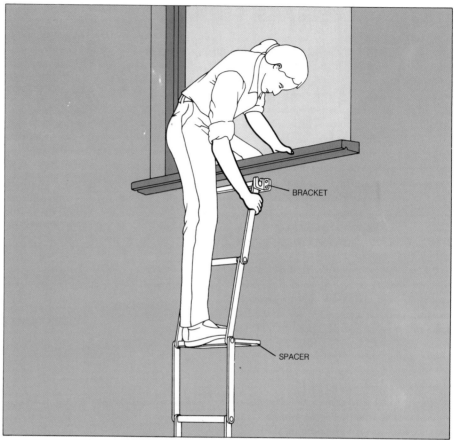

BRACKET

SPACER

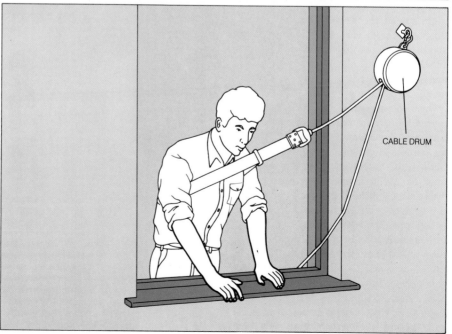

CABLE DRUM

A controlled sling. Adjacent to the window, drill a hole in the wall to take a 22 mm expanding anchor. Screw in an eye bolt with the expanding anchor attached, and secure the cable drum to the eye hook with a pompier hook. To use the sling, throw one of the two safety slings attached to the braided steel cord to the ground, then pass the second safety sling under your arms and carefully step out of the window; a geared braking mechanism in the cable drum will automatically control your rate of descent. As you drop to the ground, the first safety sling ascends to the window for the next user.

What to Do if Fire Breaks Out

When flames leap from a basement, or a smoke detector *(page 61)* clamours in the night, there is time for one thing only: escape. A quick exit from a burning house depends partly on early warning, partly on a workable escape plan.

Ideally, every room should have two possible exits, a door and a window. Each family member should know how to leave quickly and safely by every exit. Family fire drills may be necessary to practise climbing through windows, especially windows that are small and relatively inaccessible, such as those in a basement. Each drill should end at a predetermined meeting spot outside the house so that in a real fire you can tell quickly whether anyone is trapped inside. Post your plan, with exits and the meeting spot clearly marked on a floor plan of the house, where guests and baby-sitters can see it.

When a fire is detected, your first duty is to alert the other occupants of the house and make your escape. Do not try to tackle the fire yourself unless it is very small and localized *(page 97)*, and above all do not panic—this will only confuse others and increase the danger.

The safest exit route is through the front door; if the stairs and front hall are already ablaze or filled with smoke and dangerous fumes, escape from an upper window may be necessary *(page 99)*. Close all doors behind you to reduce currents of air that could spread the blaze. If you have time, telephone the fire brigade and turn off gas and electricity at the mains—but remember that escape is always the first priority, and it is usually better to telephone from a neighbour's house.

Once you are out of the building, do not return for any valuables or cherished possessions. Even though it may not seem dangerous, a sudden spread of the fire could trap you inside. Wait at a safe distance for the fire brigade to arrive.

In extreme situations—for example, the fire is already blazing and you are trapped in an upstairs room—great presence of mind is called for. Before exiting through a door, open it slightly to check for heat, flames or smoke *(right)*: opening the door in a normal fashion allows air to rush out of the room, fanning the flames and causing a sudden build-up of heat and smoke. If exit through a door is not possible, seal the gaps around it *(far right)* and then go to the window to attract the attention of people outside.

In a room filled with smoke, crawl along the floor towards the window; if possible, hold a moistened cloth over your mouth and nose. Open the window slightly and breathe through the gap until help arrives.

Never jump from a window until it is absolutely necessary. If you must jump, try to throw out a mattress or bedding to cushion the fall. Climb out of an upper window feet first with your stomach on the sill, then lower yourself down before letting go, bending your knees as you land. If the window will not open, stand back and throw a hard object through it, then pad the sill with a covering to prevent cuts as you climb through. Drop any children, if possible to an adult, before you jump.

Fire Drill for Doors

Opening a door safely. During a fire, doors must be opened only with extreme caution. Drop to a crouching position in front of the door and, with the outside of one foot placed about 50 mm from the door as a stop, open the door slightly and check your escape route. The crouching position of your body and the door itself provide protection against a possible inrush of heat and flames.

Sealing gaps. If fire traps you in a room, seal gaps around the door with blankets, curtains or a similar material. Unless there is no alternative, do not use man-made materials—these can produce toxic fumes when set alight. If water is available in the room, soak the sealing materials and swab the door with a wet cloth to prolong its resistance.

How the Pros Fight a Fire

The first rule of fire fighting—rescue the occupants—has not changed since the picturesque days of leather helmets and steam pumpers *(below)*. But other rules have been altered radically by modern research. Today, firemen attack household conflagrations with the practised skill of a well-drilled military unit assaulting an enemy position.

Unlike a home owner who douses a blaze in a wastepaper bin, the professionals do not try to extinguish extensive flames immediately. Rather, firemen initially protect what are termed the "exposures"—nearby rooms or buildings—and confine the flames to a restricted area. Only then do they begin to attack the "seat" of the fire.

Techniques for fire fighting have also been modified by research. Studies have shown that fire is generally carried by super-heated gases, rather than by the flames themselves. As gases with temperatures in excess of 760°C roll through the house, whole rooms become so hot that they spontaneously explode in a ball of flame—a phenomenon which firemen call "flashover".

To prevent flashover—and to remove heat and smoke so that firemen can get close enough to attack the fire directly—a principal weapon is not water but ventilation, which gets the super-heated gases out of the building. Therefore the professionals' method is opposite to the one recommended for an amateur: instead of closing windows to block draughts, they break window panes so that cool air from outside can replace the incendiary gases within the building.

Simultaneously with ventilation goes the use of water—sometimes mixed with chemicals—to confine and extinguish the blaze. Today, the water is seldom applied as a heavy stream, because water can cause as much property damage as the fire. Modern fire-hose nozzles can be adjusted to throw out a mist-like spray. Firemen generally fill an entire burning room with the spray, so that a thick cloud of water vapour smothers the blaze. The result is that the fire is completely extinguished with as little damage caused by the water as possible.

Fire fighting the old way. An American advertisement from the 1890s glorifies the heroic, but often misdirected, efforts of old-time firemen.

4

Coping With Everyday Hazards

A stairway made safe for all. A sturdy handrail is secured to brackets mounted on the wall to provide a firm support for the elderly or infirm on a staircase. The horizontal and sloping sections of the handrail are locked together with a handrail bolt concealed within the joint *(pages 112–114)*.

Home is second only to the car as a dangerous place to be: household accidents, including fires, kill around 6,000 Britons and injure two million each year, but fire is by no means the principal danger that lurks in a house. About 80 per cent of home mishaps are caused by mundane hazards like slippery baths and poisonous cleaners, medicines and other compounds which are kept around the house. Many of the victims are visitors to a house who are unaware of hazards that the occupants have learned to avoid.

Some accidents are .genuinely unavoidable—an elderly person who loses his balance on stairs, for example, is likely to be injured despite every effort to make the stairway safe. But you can prevent many other accidents by noticing and correcting obvious hazards. Look for accidents waiting to happen. Discard or repair pots and pans with broken or insecure handles. Make sure that sturdy steps and ladders are handy where they may be needed. Store poisons separately from medicines; segregate over-the-counter medications from prescriptions and separate medicines taken internally from those applied externally. For anyone living in the house who has poor vision, label medicine bottles, and the "on" and "off" positions of hob burner knobs, with large letters or with glued-on tactile markers—pieces of sandpaper are easy to feel.

Falls hurt more people in their homes than any other single kind of accident—causing 4,000 fatalities and 500,000 injuries in the U.K. every year. Pages 108–115 tell you how to make this type of accident less likely by mounting grab bars and applying non-slip grip strips to baths and showers, installing an additional handrail to stairways *(opposite page)* and strengthening existing banisters that have become rickety. Carpeting can add a margin of safety by improving traction on floors and stairways—and will also cushion the blow if someone should fall. If a member of your family is infirm or handicapped, there are other modifications that you can make to your house, such as a sloping ramp to an entrance doorway, extra handles for closing doors and special alterations to bathrooms and cupboards *(pages 118–123)*.

Locks and fences, which protect your home from intruders as described in Chapter 1, also work to protect you and others from a variety of dangers in and around your home. A gate at the top of a flight of stairs keeps an infant safe from falling down the stairs. Fences outdoors stop toddlers from wandering off and deter neighbourhood children who might sneak into your property *(pages 104–107)*. And lightweight locks, though they may be too flimsy to thwart a burglar, keep poisons, medicines and other household dangers safely out of the hands of youngsters *(pages 116–117)*.

Easy-to-Build Fences to Make a Garden Safe

Many home owners build fences to guard against accidents just as much as against intruders—to prevent toddlers running out of a garden, for instance, or tumbling into a swimming pool. A chain-link fence *(pages 8–13)* will meet most safety requirements, but local regulations may prohibit metal fences—and in any event, there are a number of more aesthetically pleasing alternatives available.

Before you start building any fence, make sure that you check your local building regulations. These may stipulate the fence height, its distance from the street, and who owns it when it is situated on a joint property line.

The staggered board fence shown on the following pages permits the passage of air and light while offering a considerable degree of privacy. The fence consists of 100 by 100 mm posts and vertical 150 by 25 mm boards staggered either side of 100 by 50 mm rails, with a gate built of the same materials. Use timber that has been pressure-treated to resist rot, with galvanized hardware.

Set the corner posts and gateposts in concrete to at least a quarter of their total length, making sure they are plumb; if the soil is stable, the remaining posts can be set in well-tamped soil or gravel. The posts should be no more than 2.4 metres apart, positioned so that a series of 150 by 25 mm uprights separated by a home-made spacer *(Step 3)* exactly fills the distance between posts. Once the posts are set, use a taut string to level the tops of the posts *(below)* and saw off any that are too tall. The post tops become reference points for installing fence brackets to hold the rails.

The placing of gateposts is determined by the width of the gate, which should be between 1050 and 1200 mm, plus clearance for the latch and hinges which require 12 mm and 3 mm respectively. Hang the gate so that it clears the ground through the arc of its swing.

If you want an enclosure that can be quickly dismantled, such as a dog run, the simplest method is to drive sharpened stakes into the ground and staple wire mesh to them. Wire mesh can also be strung along a balcony to prevent children falling between widely spaced railings, or it can be attached to any other fence to keep in pets. The mesh is available with a rust-resistant vinyl coating.

BRACING BOARD

GRAVEL

1 Setting the posts. Mark out the fence line and dig the holes in the same way as you would for a chain-link fence *(page 9, Step 2)*. Fill the holes with 75 mm of gravel to protect the base of the pole from damp. To set an end post, drive two stakes on adjacent sides of the hole and fasten a 50 by 25 mm bracing board to each. Place the post in the hole and plumb it for vertical using a spirit level *(above, left)*. Get a helper to hold it in position while you nail the bracing boards to the post. Brace the other end post in the same way. Align the intermediate posts with two lengths of string stretched between the end posts, at the top and bottom of the fence *(above, right)*. Adjust the height of the posts by adding or removing gravel until they are aligned. Use bracing boards to keep the posts vertical and fill the holes with concrete as shown on page 10, Step 4.

BRACKET

2 **Hanging the rails.** Slide 100 by 50 mm rails into metal fence-rail brackets mounted on the fence posts, placing the upper brackets 250 mm down from the tops of the posts; ensure each bracket is level by using a try square to draw a line across the post and aligning the bottom of the bracket against it. To position lower brackets, measure down from the top of one post to about 150 mm from the ground; use this measurement to draw lines for the lower brackets on all the other posts. Nail the rails to the brackets.

To make a spacer for positioning fence boards, cut a piece of 100 by 25 mm board to the length of the fence boards. Scribe a line 150 mm from one end of the spacer and nail a block of wood to the spacer, the bottom of the block on the line.

3 **Spacing the boards.** Hold a 150 by 25 mm fence board against the rails, with one edge of the board touching a post and the top of the board aligned with the post top; nail the board to the rails. Hook the spacer over the upper rail, using the block as a hanger, and slide the spacer against the first board. Hold a second board against the other side of the spacer, align it and nail it in place. Continue in this way to attach boards to the rails, using the spacer and occasionally checking a board for plumb by holding a level against it.

When one side of the fence is completed, similarly space and fasten boards to the other side of the fence. On this side, however, centre the first board between the first two boards on the side you have completed.

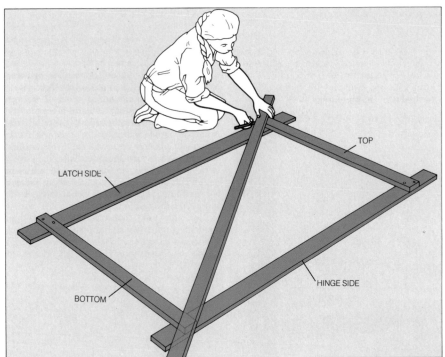

4 **Making the gate.** Construct a frame for the gate from two 100 by 50 mm rails cut to fit loosely between the gateposts, two 150 by 25 mm fence boards and a diagonal 100 by 50 mm brace. Assemble these elements so the gate rails line up with the rails on the completed fence, using a square to make sure the corners form right angles. Cut the diagonal brace to fit between the two rails, running from the top of the latch side to the bottom of the hinge side. Fasten the brace to the frame with 100 mm wood screws, two at each end, driving the screws through the brace into the edges of the rails.

Nail fence boards on to the outside of the gate, leaving 3 mm between the boards. Then screw the strap sections of two socket hinges on to the top and bottom gate rails.

5 **Hanging the gate.** Mark the positions of the screws for hinges by propping the gate between its posts, using scrap timber to hold it in position. Align the top of the gate with the top of the fence and set the gate frame flush with the backs of the posts. Starting with the bottom hinge, slot the spindles into the sockets, mark fixing positions for them on the gatepost, then drill the holes and screw the spindles in position. Nail a 25 by 25 mm piece of timber to the post opposite the hinges to act as a stop.

To install the thumb latch *(inset)*, drill a vertical slot near the edge of the top rail of the gate; screw the thumb plate to the outside of the gate, so that the lever goes through and rests on the bottom of the slot. Attach the rising bar to the gate so that it rests on top of the protruding lever, then fix the latching bracket to the gatepost. Make sure that when the lever is raised from either side of the gate, the rising bar will clear the latching bracket, enabling the gate to open.

Stepping Down a Slope

1 **Marking out the posts.** Drive in a tall stake at the bottom of the slope and run a string to it from ground level at the top of the slope. Level the string with a water level. The height from ground level of the string on the stake is the vertical drop of the hill; to calculate the individual section drop, divide the number of fence sections between posts into the total vertical drop. For a very long or steep hill, carry out the procedure in instalments and total the measurements.

Cut a gauge pole to the distance between post centres. Working with a helper, measure along the string with the gauge pole and drop a plumb bob to mark the post locations, driving marker stakes into the ground (*below*).

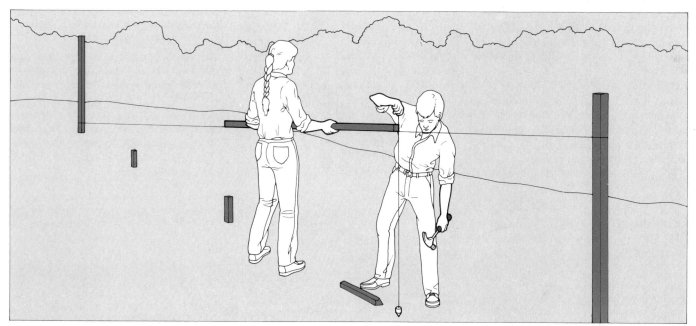

2 **Attaching the rails and boards.** Install the top post to the intended fence height, then set the rest of the posts to the fence height plus the section drop. Secure the upper rail bracket to the bottom post 250 mm from the top, then secure the corresponding bracket to the second post, checking for level with a spirit level and line. Secure the lower bracket to the second post about 150 mm from the ground, then secure the corresponding bracket to the bottom post, again checking for level. Slide the upper and lower rails into the brackets. Fit the brackets and rails between the remaining posts in the same way. To secure the uprights, rest each board on the ground; hold it away from the previous board with a spacer (*page 105, Step 3*) and nail it to the rails. When each section is complete, mark a line across the top of the boards and saw them off level.

Defusing the Dangers of Bathrooms and Stairs

Accidental injuries occur more often in the home than anywhere else. Most household accidents are of the roller-skate-on-the-stairs variety—avoidable by using common sense. Others may be caused by the design of a house—a kitchen extension one step down from the main floor or a raised dining area one step up lead to countless wrenched ankles.

Still other accidents occur despite good design and common caution—bathrooms and staircases, which are responsible for many injuries in the home, are dangerous even if they are built correctly and used with care. But there are things you can do to make these two areas of the house safer.

Staircases are discussed in detail on pages 110–115. In bathrooms, the major cause of accidents is a slippery bath or shower tray. Textured grip strips, sometimes sold in pre-cut lengths, can be stuck to the bottom of a bath or to the floor of a shower tray to help reduce this danger. Rubber bath mats are a popular alternative; they must be dried after use to prevent perishing. For other slippery areas (in front of a sink or a washing machine for example) there is a heavy-duty, self-adhesive tape made of rubber latex compound with a textured surface.

The durability of such non-slip surfaces depends largely on the smoothness and cleanliness of the surface beneath. Wash the surface thoroughly, scraping off any old or curled strips with a putty knife and a solvent such as alcohol or lacquer thinner. Then lay out a pattern for the strips and stick them in place as shown below and at the top of the opposite page.

Even with grip strips, however, you can still slip and fall. To lessen that risk, install grab rails *(opposite page, below)* to provide hand holds. Buy special grab rails—even the strongest of towel rails may give way. They should be at least 450 mm long, free of sharp corners and welded in one strong piece so that vulnerable areas are limited to the two fixing points.

Creating a Slip-Resistant Surface

Patterns for grip strips. In a shower *(right, above)*, lay grip strips in a star pattern radiating from the centre of the shower floor. This pattern encourages the waste water to run towards the drain. Use six full-length strips for the long rays and three strips cut in half for the short rays. Round corners so they will not curl. In a bath *(right, below)*, centre a wedge for four full-length strips round the plughole, then add three strips at the other end of the bath, parallel to the sides.

For a non-slip surface in front of a sink or a washing machine, cut 500 mm lengths of 25 mm wide heavy-duty rubber latex tape. Arrange strips of tape 75 mm apart and parallel to the front edge of the sink or washing machine and round the corners.

Installing grip strips. Peel away 25 mm of the paper backing and stick the end of the strip to the surface. Slowly peel off the backing and press the strip against the surface. Finally, press the strip with a wallpaper-seam roller.

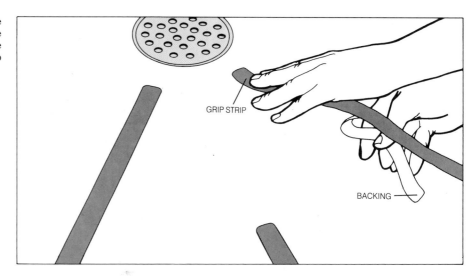

GRIP STRIP

BACKING

Grab Rails for Shower and Bath

1 Positioning grab rails. On the wall of a shower cubicle or next to a bath, centre a grab rail at a convenient height and angle. If you have to drill through tiles, temporarily attach a piece of thin card or strips of masking tape behind each flange and mark screw holes on to the card or tape *(right)*. Using a masonry bit on a hammer-action drill, make holes for 50 mm No. 10 plugs and screws. Apply light pressure and drill at low speed to avoid breaking the tiles, then peel the tape or card from the wall.

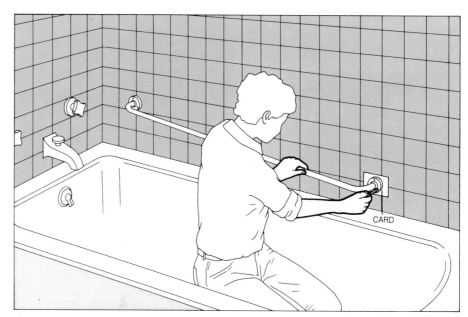

CARD

2 Fastening the grab rail. Plug the holes, then attach each bracket to the wall with either chromium-plated brass or stainless steel screws. Tighten all the screws and pull strongly on the rail to check that it is firmly secured.

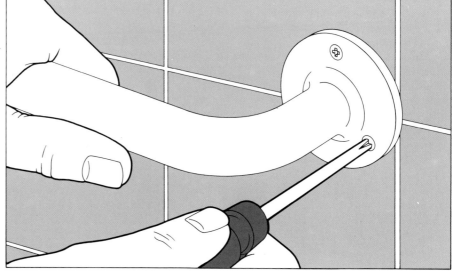

For Staircases, Firm Handholds

Staircases are the most dangerous part of a house, surpassing even bathrooms as a site of accidents. Some stairs have trouble built into them. They can be too steep. Tall or uneven risers invite climbers to trip on tread nosings. Shallow treads make stairs difficult to descend without catching a heel on a riser or slipping over a nosing. Staircases with these deficiencies cannot be made safe; the stairs should be replaced. Other unsafe staircases have no risers at all, but the danger of catching a foot between treads can be eliminated by nailing risers to the boards that support the treads.

Even a well-designed staircase is no guarantee against accidents. The steps may be treacherously slippery; the newel posts, which anchor the balustrade, may have loosened with age. And very few staircases are built with a handrail on the stairway wall, a basic safeguard against a fall. All of these hazards should be corrected by the methods described below.

The most slippery stairs are those with a natural finish. If you insist on the beauty of bare wood, use non-slip polish on your stairs. It is safer to cover them up with something less slippery. If you choose carpeting, use a low-pile variety—it is less likely to catch a heel or to make a tread seem wider than it is. Unless you are confident of your carpeting skills, have the job done professionally: carpeting that is poorly installed is more hazardous than no carpeting at all. Carpeting should be pulled tight round the nosings and fixed securely with heavy-duty staples tucked well into the back of the tread. On basement or attic stairs, where the luxury of carpet may be inappropriate, tack rubber safety treads to the wooden ones, apply heavy-duty grip strips (pages 108–109) to treads or coat the treads with paint that contains pumice.

A balustrade will often begin to wobble when the joint between the newel post and string—the long board running up the outside of the staircase and supporting the steps—has become damaged. Tighten this joint by driving screws through the newel into the string (opposite page, above).

If a staircase is more than a metre wide, it is wise to mount a sturdy handrail on the wall beside the stairs, using metal brackets (page 112). You will need three brackets for each straight section of stair—placed at the top, centre and bottom of the rail—and additional brackets for each turn. The height of the rail should be between 840 mm and 1 metre vertically above the pitch line, the angle of ascent as defined by the nosing of each tread. The rail should reach from the top landing to the nosing of the bottom tread, though you may shorten it by a step without risk.

Handrails are made in a range of woods, from a plain circular shaft of softwood known as "mopstick" to expensive decorative hardwood. Order one that measures no more than 75 mm at its widest; wider rails are difficult to grasp.

To shape the ends of a straight length of handrail, simply round off the sharp edges. Alternatively, buy a short curved section called a ramp-piece. Joined to the end of the handrail, this piece will level the rail at the landing (page 115, Step 9). Other curved sections can also be used to take the handrail round corners and up another flight of stairs.

Join sections of handrail with two glued dowels and a handrail screw, a special connecting device that is threaded at both ends. One end serves as an ordinary wood screw; the other has a nut and functions as a bolt. Attach the first two sections of handrail at a workbench (page 114, Step 8). Prepare the joints for additional sections as described on pages 113–114, Steps 5, 6 and 7, and install them with the rail fixed to the wall.

With a second handrail in place, the stairs are as safe as possible for everyone except crawling or toddling children. To stop them from tumbling down the stairs, close off the top of the staircase with an expanding gate (page 115).

Securing a Loose Newel

Screwing a newel to the string. On the front of the newel post base, make marks for two screws, one above the other. Measure carefully to ensure that the screws will be in line with the end of the string on the opposite side of the post. Using an electric drill fitted with a 12 mm spade bit, bore two countersunk holes 20 mm deep at these marks. Extend them through the newel with shank holes for No. 12 screws, then, using a large screwdriver, drive two screws at least 100 mm long through the holes and into the string *(inset)*. Plug the holes with sections of dowelling or cross-grain pellets.

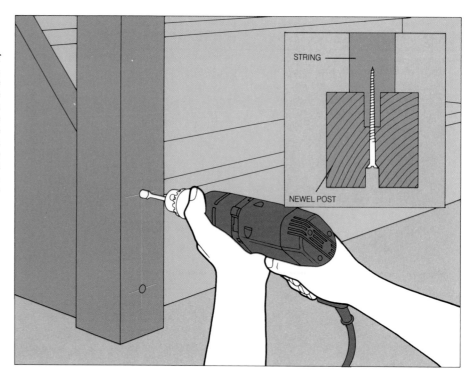

Adding a Rail to a Stairway Wall

1 Positioning brackets. Measure the vertical distance from the nosing of the bottom tread to the underside of the existing handrail. Transfer the measurement, less the height of a handrail bracket, to the wall above the bottom tread nosing and above the upper landing nosing. With a helper, snap a chalk line between these points.

Make marks 150 mm in from the top and bottom end of the chalk line for two of the brackets, and make a third mark midway along the line for the third bracket. Mark for additional brackets wherever your handrail is jointed for a turn or for levelling off at a landing.

2 **Securing brackets to the wall.** Place the bottom edge of a handrail bracket over each mark on the chalk line and mark the positions for screw holes. Drill holes for No. 10 plugs, and secure each bracket with 37 to 50 mm No. 10 screws.

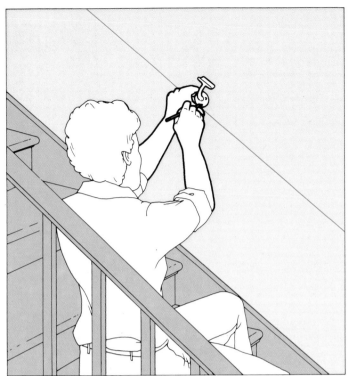

3 **Fitting the handrail.** Lay a length of handrail on the stairs against the wall, aligning the bottom end with the bottom nosing. For a single, straight length of handrail, mark the top end of the rail directly above the top nosing. Cut the end with a tenon saw in a mitre box to ensure a square cut, and smooth the sawn end with sandpaper. Fit the rail as described on page 115, Step 9.

4 **Trimming the ramp-piece.** After aligning the handrail as in Step 3, place the ramp-piece against the handrail so that the curve is aligned with the top nosing. Mark the handrail along the lower end of the ramp-piece and cut along this line, using a tenon saw in a mitre box.

5 **Marking for the joint.** Draw a line across the end of the rail at its widest part, and make three equally spaced marks to establish the position of the screw and dowels *(inset)*. Tap 25 mm panel pins into the marks. Snap the heads of the pins off at an angle with pincers. Lay the handrail and ramp-piece end to end on their sides, holding a batten firmly against their undersides. Push the ends together hard enough for the panel pins to make marks in the ramp-piece.

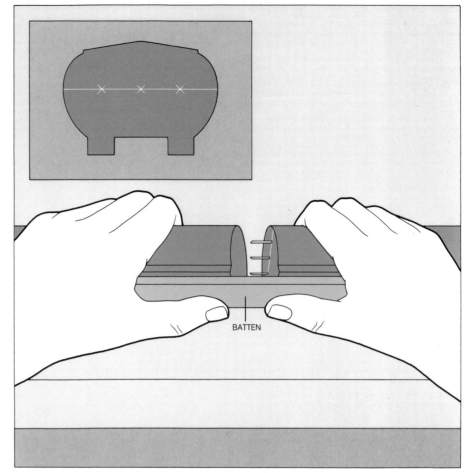

BATTEN

6 **Drilling for the screw and dowels.** Place the hand-rail in a cramp between two scraps of wood and remove the panel pins. At the two outer marks drill holes 6 mm in diameter and 30 mm deep for the dowels. At the centre mark, drill a shank hole for the bolt end of the handrail screw. Put the ramp-piece in the cramp and drill matching dowel holes at the outer marks. In the centre, drill a pilot hole for the wood screw end of the handrail screw *(right)*.

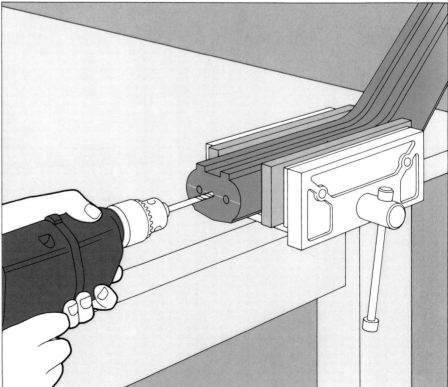

7 **Cutting an access hole.** Clamp the handrail upside down and mark the outline for a square access hole, centred 20 mm from the end of the rail. The hole must be 10 mm wider than the castellated nut that will fit on the bolt end of the handrail screw. Holding a wood chisel at a slight angle, make a series of deep cuts across the face of the outline. Then turn the chisel round and cut back across the notch. Continue working back and forth across the outlined area until the depth of the hole is slightly below the shank hole of the handrail screw *(inset)*. Drop the nut into the access hole and check that there is enough room for the bolt end of the screw to pick up the nut. Make similar access holes for other joints along your projected handrail.

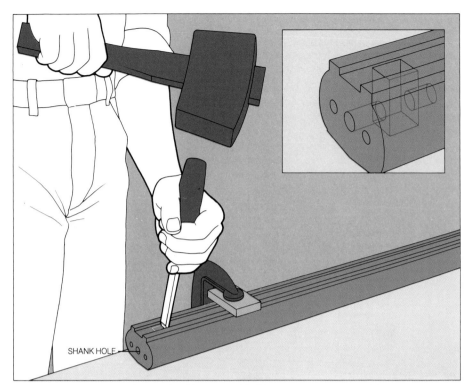

SHANK HOLE

8 **Joining the ramp-piece to the handrail.** Using pliers, wind the wood screw end of the handrail screw fully into the ramp-piece. With a tenon saw, cut a shallow groove along the lengths of two 30 mm pieces of 6 mm dowel. Squeeze PVA adhesive into all four dowel holes, and push the dowels into the dowel holes in the ramp-piece. Smear adhesive over the ends of the rail and ramp-piece, drop the nut into the access hole and push the two pieces together. When the bolt and the nut engage, wind the nut on to the bolt with a screwdriver or nail punch angled against the nut's castellated edges *(right)*; continue turning until the joint is completely closed. Fill the hole with a piece of wood cut to size.

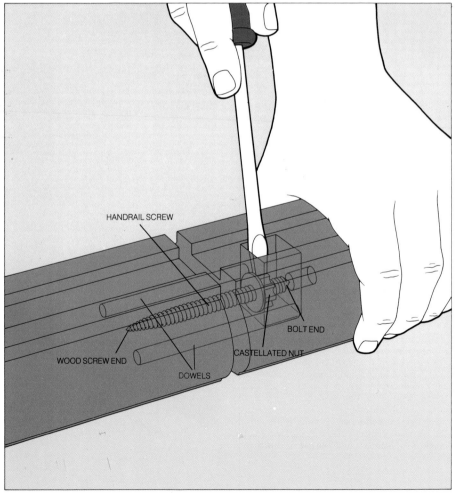

HANDRAIL SCREW

BOLT END

CASTELLATED NUT

WOOD SCREW END

DOWELS

9 **Installing the rail.** With the aid of a helper, set the rail on the brackets and mark the positions for screws on the underside of the rail. Remove the rail and drill pilot holes. Lift the rail back on to the brackets, and secure it in place with 25 mm No. 8 screws *(inset)*.

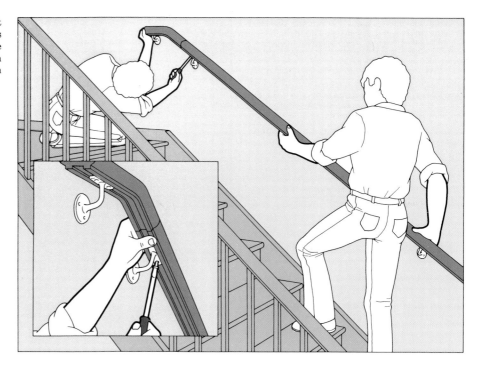

A Safety Gate to Protect Toddlers

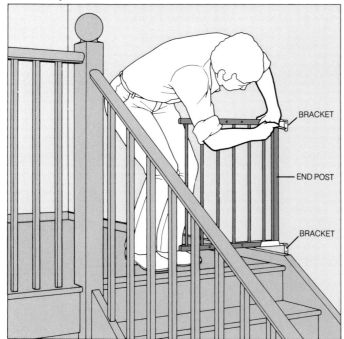

BRACKET

END POST

BRACKET

STRIKE PLATE

CATCH

1 **Attaching the gate.** Fit a bracket to the bottom of the end post of the gate and set it against the newel post or just above the skirting. Mark the location for screw holes, remove the bracket from the gate and set the gate aside. Attach the bracket to the wall with 37 mm No. 8 wood screws. Set the gate in the bottom bracket and fit a bracket to the top of the end post. Mark a hole for the upper bracket and attach it with the gate in position.

2 **Installing the catch.** Assemble the gate, extend it to the width of your staircase and install the catch according to the manufacturer's instructions; where possible, locate the catch on the staircase side of the gate so that a child cannot release it. Install the strike plate on the wall or newel post *(above)*.

Keeping Knives and Poisons Out of Reach

In past centuries, a proper housewife wore a ring of keys befitting a gaoler, to lock up everything from tea canisters and canteens of silver to cupboards of clothes. Those parlous times are gone, but even today the contents of some cabinets and drawers need simple safeguards. In a household with children, you can keep knives, medicines and poisonous products out of reach with a concealed safety latch screwed inside a wooden cabinet or glued to a metal one; the model on the right, above, has an ingenious hook fastening that is proof against most youngsters but opens at the touch of an adult's finger.

Elsewhere, a cabinet or a chest of drawers may need a true lock to guard its contents. For a cabinet with sliding glass doors, a showcase lock *(right, below)* of the kind used in jewellery shops is adequate, and no lock is easier to install—it simply clamps into place. A cabinet with swinging doors can be fitted with an attractive hasp *(opposite page, above)* that is available with a locking cam rather than a separate padlock. Like a standard hasp-and-padlock assembly, this lock is screwed to the outside of a door.

Installing a recessed drawer lock *(opposite page, below)* is more involved, and demands some of the intricate joinery used for the lock of a door. Besides a screwdriver, you will need a spade bit to bore a hole for the lock barrel and a wood chisel to cut mortises for the lock plate, lock housing and strike plate.

Childproofing a cabinet. To install this widely available latch, screw the catch inside the cabinet top, no more than 25 mm from the side, projecting inwards. Hook the latch in the centre of the shaft under the catch and mark the location of the shaft base on the inside of the door. Fasten the shaft to the door. The latch will engage the catch when the door is closed; you release the latch by opening the door just wide enough to slip a finger over the top, then pushing the shaft down and out of the catch—a trick few young children can master. For a recessed or overhanging cabinet, reverse the mounting of the shaft and set it about 25 mm from the front edge, so that the latch at the end engages the catch *(inset)*. The door should not open more than 30 mm.

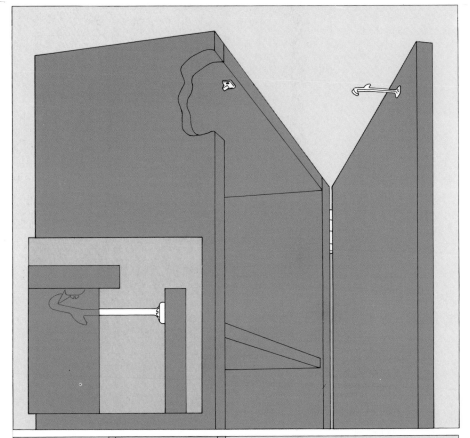

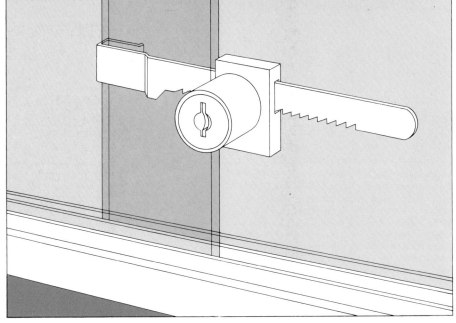

Attaching a showcase lock. With the doors open, slip the hook of the lock bar round the edge of the inner door, with the serrated edge of the bar pointing down. Close the doors and slide the lock barrel on to the bar until the barrel is flush with the edge of the outside door. The lock cannot be removed, nor the doors opened, until you unlock the barrel with a key.

Installing a hasp lock. Measure the distance between the centres of the hasp hinge pin and the hasp opening and mark the face of one cabinet door at a point that is half this distance from the edge of the door. Set the hasp against the door, with its hinge pin centred over the mark; mark the screw holes and attach the hasp to the door. Set the lock against the adjoining door with the cam of the lock protruding through the hasp opening, mark the positions of the lock's screw holes and fasten the lock to the door. You can secure the hasp to the lock by turning the cam 90 degrees with your fingers; to return it to the "open" position, you must use a key.

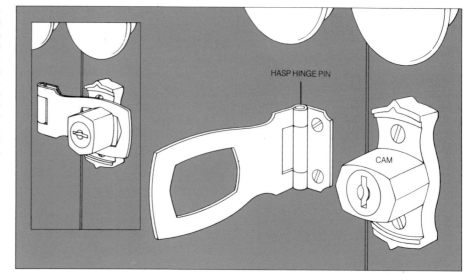

A Recessed Drawer Lock

1 Mounting the lock. To install this lock, you must bore a hole through the drawer front for the barrel; cut a mortise, or recess, in the top of the drawer front for the flange of the fixing plate above the barrel; and cut another mortise in the back of the drawer front for the housing at the base of the barrel (the drawing on the right shows the third part of the job).

Start by measuring the distance from the top of the flange to the centre of the barrel *(inset)*, mark this distance down from the top of the drawer and, at the mark, drill a hole through the drawer front for the barrel. Insert the barrel from inside the drawer, mark the length of the flange on the drawer top and cut the flange mortise. Reinsert the barrel, outline the fixing plate and cut its mortise. Expand both mortises to take the barrel housing until the lock fits snugly, then screw the lock in place from inside the drawer.

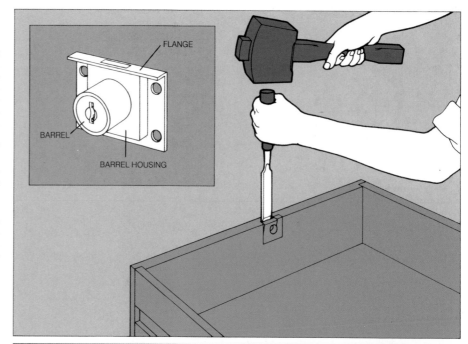

2 Mounting the strike plate. Rub chalk or lipstick along the top of the bolt, close the drawer fully and use the key to wind out the bolt until it presses against the cabinet top. Remove the drawer and, at the mark, cut a hole deep enough to seat the bolt fully *(inset);* then set the strike plate over the hole, trace its outline and cut a mortise for it. Screw the plate to the cabinet.

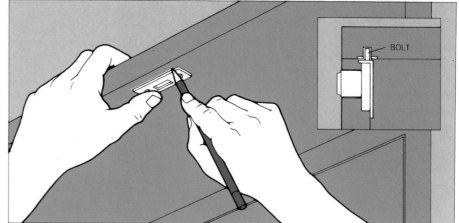

Adapting a House to the Needs of the Infirm

Making your house safe and secure for a physically handicapped or infirm member of the family—without inconveniencing the others in the house—can be as simple as swapping bedrooms, shifting shelves in a wardrobe *(opposite page, above)*, or re-arranging furniture to provide clearance for a walking frame or a wheelchair (750 mm for passage, 1500 mm for turning round). More extensive changes pay dividends and involve only basic carpentry.

Among the simplest conveniences to add are grab rails *(page 109)*. Mounted on doors, they make it easier for a person in a wheelchair to pull the door closed *(below)*; and they are essential in a bathroom *(page 120)*. For someone confined to a wheelchair, a shower cubicle with an access ramp may be easier to negotiate than a bath, in which case the grab rail needs to be installed at wheelchair height as shown on the opposite page, below.

Working in a kitchen can pose serious problems for someone in a wheelchair. There are many aids for specific tasks, but the first priority is plenty of space and low work surfaces *(page 120)*. Other disabilities may require different adaptations. Before starting work, contact your local council to find out if a kitchen or bathroom adaptation qualifies for a grant.

Eliminating the biggest obstacle that the handicapped face at home—steps—requires a ramp to turn a steep rise into a gentle incline. Few houses have room for a ramp indoors, but there is often space for one outside, where steps lead from a door into the garden.

Because of its strength and durability, concrete is widely used as a ramp-building material. The plywood structure on pages 121–123 is easy both to put up and to take down—an important consideration if ever you wish to sell your house.

Bear in mind, however, that the maximum length of a sheet of plywood is 3660 mm, which means that if your ramp is going to be longer than this, it will have to consist of more than one section. The plywood structure shown on pages 121–123 is comprised of three sections—an upper ramp, a lower ramp and a level landing—each fitted with handrails and knee rails. These basic components can be used in a number of permutations. By placing a landing between two ramp sections, for example, you can make one of the sections turn a corner or double back on the other.

Such combinations are invaluable where you need to reach a high doorway, but wish to avoid making the ramp either too long or too steep. In fact, the recommended gradient for a ramp is 1:12, and the maximum acceptable length without a rest platform is 10 metres. Like the landing at the top of the ramp, rest platforms should be at least 1800 mm long, so that a person in a wheelchair need have no fear of rolling backwards down the slope.

The width of each section, including ramp, landing and any rest platforms, should ideally not be less than 1200 mm. It is easiest, therefore, to use the plywood sheets that come in widths of 1220 mm. This is wide enough for a wheelchair to pass comfortably, and narrow enough for the person in the chair to grasp the handrails. These should be between 840 and 1000 mm above ramp level; and knee rails should be at an equal distance between the ramp and the handrails.

Buy pressure-treated timber and soak the sawn ends with wood preservative before assembling the ramp. To prevent the ramp surface from becoming slippery in wet weather, coat it with abrasive paint.

The most satisfactory base for a ramp of this type is gravel, but any flat surface is adequate. If the ground is level, the ramp will be held in place by its own weight.

Dealing with Doors

Mounting a grab rail and kick plates. Mount a grab rail 750 mm above the floor on the side of the door that swings into the doorway, so that a person in a wheelchair can use the rail to pull the door closed. On a solid-core door, secure the rail with 32 mm wood screws; on a hollow-core door, either attach the rail with toggle-fixing screws or use 32 mm wood screws driven into the stiles.

Screw metal or plastic kick plates at the bottom of the door to prevent scuffing from wheelchair footrests or walking frames. On a hollow-core door, screw the kick plates to the stiles, or use contact adhesive.

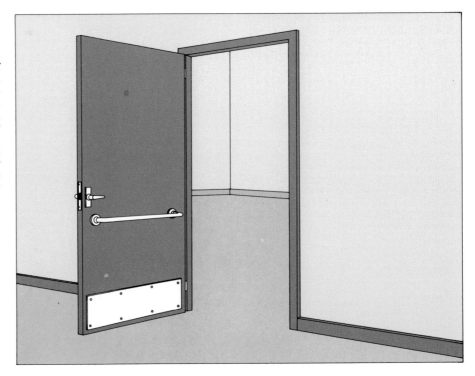

Arranging Clothes for Easy Access

Adapting a wardrobe. Partition the hanging part of the wardrobe into two sections, fixing the clothes rail of one section some 1050 mm above floor level to allow easy access from a wheelchair. Fix the clothes rail in the other section a little higher so that items such as dresses and over-coats can be hung full-length. Install a shelf about 150 mm above the lower rail and no more than 400 mm deep; this will enable someone in a wheelchair to reach objects stored at the back of the shelf. Make sure that any drawers accessible from a wheelchair are shallow and easy to open. Swing-out shelf units and a shoe tidy attached to the inside of a door are other useful accessories.

A Bathroom and Shower for the Elderly or Disabled

Adapting a shower. Ramped on two sides for either walk-in or wheelchair access, this shower is fitted with a fold-back shower seat, an easy-to-reach grab rail *(page 109)* and a thermostatic mixer unit with single-lever control for both water flow and temperature. The spray can be adjusted simply by sliding or pivoting the shower nozzle on its rail.

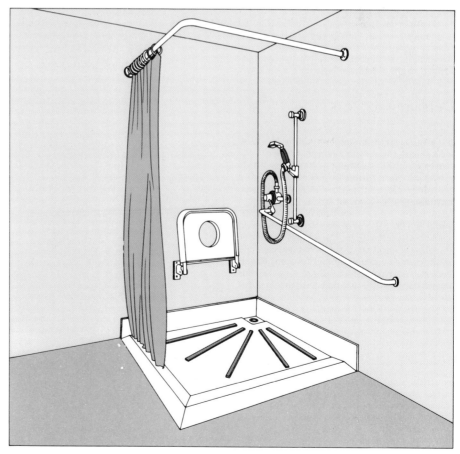

Adapting a bathroom. Install grab rails next to the bath and W.C.; the grab rails for the bath must be fixed to the wall, but the rails for the W.C. can be fixed to either the seat, the wall or the floor. To assist a handicapped person getting in and out of the bath, place a board across the top of the bath and an adjustable seat inside. A pedestal wash basin gives better access than one that is recessed into a vanity unit; and lever-type taps should be fitted on both the bath and wash basin. Fit a long mirror immediately above the sink, so that it can be used by all members of the family—including the person in the wheelchair.

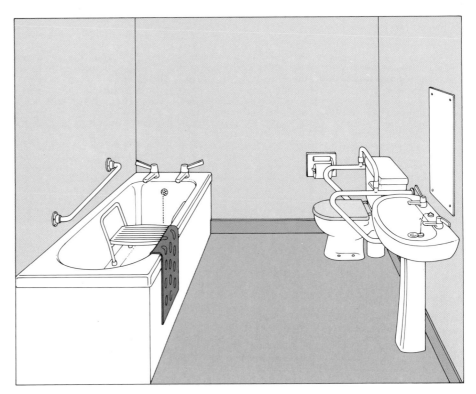

Making the Kitchen More Accessible

Choosing the right fixtures. For a person in a wheelchair, the kitchen needs to be spacious, allowing plenty of legroom beneath the sink and the worktops. At the same time, these units should be at a comfortable working level, generally no more than about 775 mm above the floor. The sink shown here can be raised or lowered simply by touching a lever. Where fixed worktops are insufficient, install pull-out worktops, either solid or with cut-outs for mixing bowls.

Whatever the disability, overhead cupboards are usually inaccessible. A number of specially designed storage fittings are available instead, including shallow carousel shelves for corner cupboards, and trolley units that fit beneath work surfaces. Other useful devices are door-mounted waste bins and telescopic towel rails. Beading at the edges of worktops can prevent breakages and spills while a guard fixed round the oven hob will keep pots and pans from falling. An oven door that is hinged at the side may be easier for a disabled person to cope with than one that is hinged at the bottom. Either way, make sure that the door is adequately insulated.

For those with hand disabilities, D-shaped handles are usually the easiest to grasp. However, if these are also a problem, you can try fitting them with large, easy-to-pull loops. Special electrical plugs with handles are also available. As for the sockets, these should be placed just above work surfaces, where they can be reached without bending or stretching.

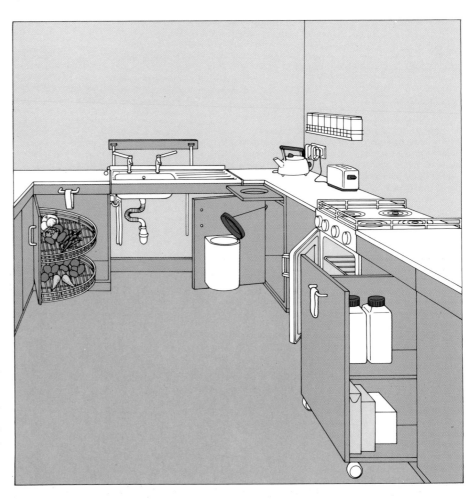

A Ramp for a Wheelchair

1 **Fitting battens and bearers.** Using 18 mm thick exterior-grade plywood, cut two pairs of wedge-shaped strings—the first for the upper part of the ramp and the second for the lower section *(inset)*. Lay the upper strings on the ground, with the outer sides uppermost, and drill pilot holes at 200 mm intervals along three edges; do not drill holes in the short edge.

Place 50 by 50 mm battens under the strings along the long edges, and secure them with 50 mm No. 10 galvanized screws *(below)*. Screw a 50 by 50 mm bearer between the battens, in line with the longer of the vertical edges. Make all screw heads flush with the surface.

Fix battens and bearers to the lower strings in the same way, shaping the lower ends of the battens so that they will sit flush on the ground *(page 122, Step 3, inset)*.

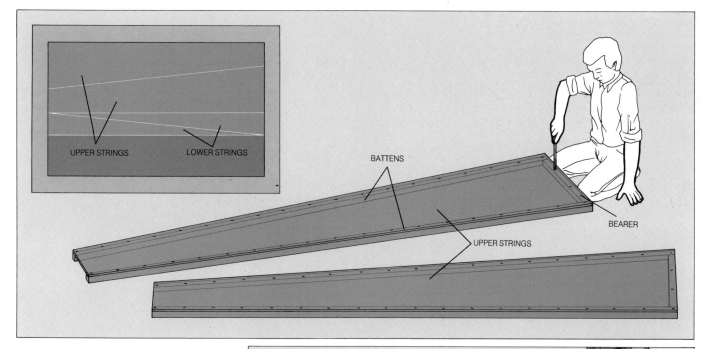

UPPER STRINGS   LOWER STRINGS

BATTENS

BEARER

UPPER STRINGS

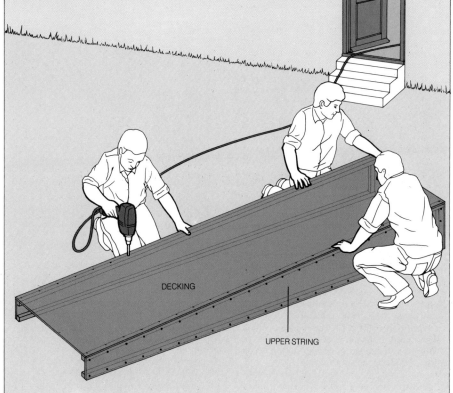

DECKING

UPPER STRING

2 **Fitting the decking.** Use a sheet of plywood at least 1000 mm wide for the upper ramp decking and get a couple of helpers to hold the upper strings plumb while you fix the decking to the battens. Drill pilot holes at 200 mm intervals along the edges of the decking *(right)* and secure with 50 mm No. 10 galvanized screws, as described in Step 1, above. Use a second sheet of plywood of the same width for the lower ramp decking and fit this to the lower strings.

3 **Assembling the framework.** Turn over the upper section of ramp, so that the lower battens are on top, and cut 50 by 50 mm spreaders to fit between them, one at each end and the others at 600 mm intervals. Drill pilot holes through the strings and battens, then secure the spreaders with 100 mm No. 10 galvanized screws, making the heads flush with the surface. Fix spreaders between the upper battens in the same way, except at the lower end.

Turn the ramp the right way up *(right)* and drill pilot holes at 180 mm intervals across its width, 25 mm from the lower edge. Cut a 100 by 50 mm joining bearer to fit between the lower ends of the upper battens. Leaving 50 mm proud of the edge, insert the joining bearer and secure with 50 mm No. 10 galvanized screws, making the heads flush with the surface.

Turn over the lower section of ramp and install spreaders in the same way as for the upper section; fit the lowest one just above the point where the battens have been shaped to rest flush on the ground *(inset)*.

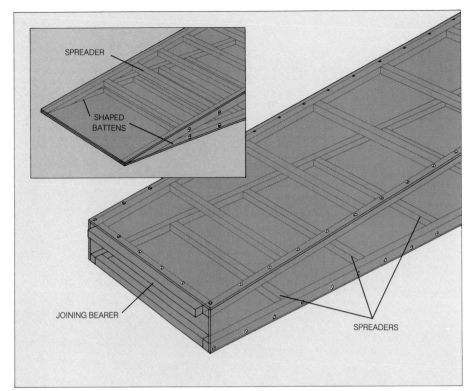

SPREADER

SHAPED BATTENS

JOINING BEARER

SPREADERS

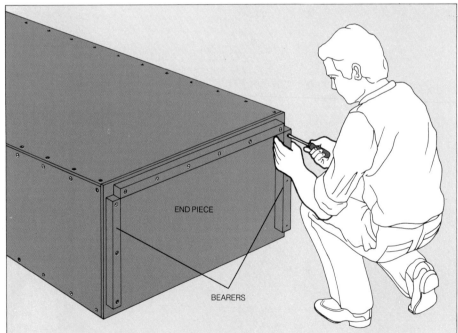

END PIECE

BEARERS

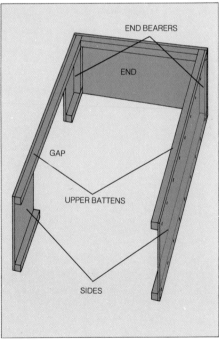

END BEARERS

END

GAP

UPPER BATTENS

SIDES

4 **Completing the ramp.** Push the two ramp sections together and drill pilot holes at 180 mm intervals across the width of the lower section, 25 mm in from the upper edge. Use 50 mm No. 10 galvanized screws to fix the lower section to the joining bearer of the upper section.

From 1220 mm wide plywood, cut a piece to fit the end of the upper ramp section. Drill pilot holes at 200 mm intervals along the top and sides of the end piece and secure it to the underlying edge of the ramp decking and the bearers

of the upper strings. Fix with 50 mm No. 10 galvanized screws, making the heads flush with the surface.

Using 50 by 50 mm timber, fix an upper batten and two bearers to the end piece, 18 mm in from the edge *(above)*. Leave a 68 mm gap on either side of the batten and above the bearers, and a 50 mm gap below the bearers. Drill pilot holes at 200 mm intervals along the batten and bearers, this time securing with 68 mm No. 10 galvanized screws.

5 **Making the landing.** Cut sections of plywood for an end, a top and two sides. Fit 50 by 50 mm battens to the sides; fit an upper batten and two bearers to the end *(page 121, Step 1)*. Leave a 68 mm gap on either side of the end batten, and a 50 mm gap above and below the end bearers. Cut a gap in the section—in this case, one of the sides—to be fitted over the steps. With 50 mm No. 10 galvanized screws, fix the sides to the end bearers; fix the top to the upper battens of the end and the sides.

6 **Joining the ramp and the landing.** Push the landing into position against the wall, then move the ramp into position next to the landing. Drill pilot holes at 180 mm intervals along the top and side of the landing, 25 mm from the edge, and use 50 mm No. 10 galvanized screws to fix the landing to the batten and bearers of the ramp end piece installed in Step 4.

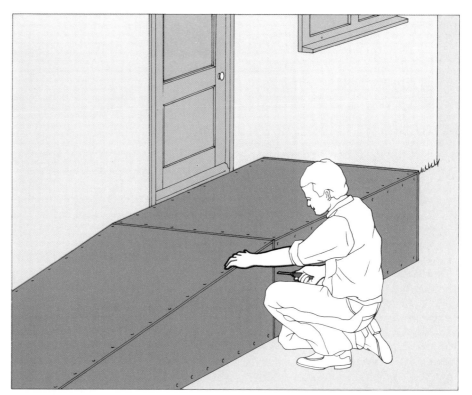

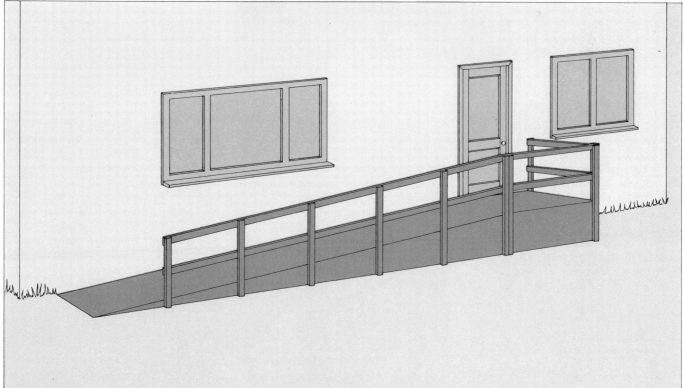

7 **Fixing the rails.** Using 100 by 50 mm timber, cut posts to stand between 840 and 1000 mm above ramp level. Secure the posts to the upper and lower battens of the ramp and landing, inserting two 10 mm coach screws into each post; fit two pairs of adjoining posts—one at the top of the ramp where it meets the landing, and the other at the outside corner of the landing.

Using 100 by 37 mm timber, cut three sections of handrail—one for the ramp, and one for each exposed side of the landing. Plane and sand down any roughness, then fasten the rails to the insides of the posts, using two 50 mm No. 10 galvanized screws at each post. Drill pilot holes and counter-sink the screw heads. Cut and install a knee rail in the same way, positioning it an equal distance between the ramp and the handrail.

If the width of the ramp exceeds 1000 mm and the height is more than 600 mm, attach a handrail to the wall.

Picture Credits

The sources for the illustrations in this book are shown below. Credits for the illustrations from left to right are separated by semicolons, from top to bottom by dashes.

Cover: John Elliott. 6: John Elliott. 8–12: Drawings by Hayward and Martin Limited. 13: Drawing by Hayward and Martin Limited—drawings by John Massey. 15–17: Drawings by Hayward and Martin Limited. 18: Drawing by Frederic F. Bigio from B-C Graphics. 19–21: Drawings by Hayward and Martin Limited. 22: Drawing by Hayward and Martin Limited; drawings by Frederic F. Bigio from B-C Graphics. 23, 24: Drawings by Hayward and Martin Limited. 25: Drawings by Frederic F. Bigio from B-C Graphics. 26–37: Drawings by Hayward and Martin Limited. 38: Drawings by Peter McGinn. 39: Drawings by Hayward and Martin Limited. 41: Drawings by Frederic F. Bigio from B-C Graphics—drawings by Hayward and Martin Limited; drawing by Frederic F. Bigio from B-C Graphics. 42–45: Drawings by Frederic F. Bigio from B-C Graphics. 47: Drawing by Hayward and Martin Limited. 48: Drawings by Frederic F. Bigio from B-C Graphics. 49: Drawings by Frederic F. Bigio from B-C Graphics—Courtesy the Lincoln Electric Company. 50: Drawings by Frederic F. Bigio from B-C Graphics. 51: Drawing by Frederic F. Bigio from B-C Graphics—drawing by Hayward and Martin Limited. 52, 53: Drawings by Frederic F. Bigio from B-C Graphics. 54: Drawing by Hayward and Martin Limited. 55: Drawings by Frederic F. Bigio from B-C Graphics. 56: Fil Hunter. 58, 59: Drawings by Hayward and Martin Limited. 60: Drawing by Hayward and Martin Limited—drawing by Gerry Gallagher. 61: Drawings by Gerry Gallagher. 62–65: Drawings by Hayward and Martin Limited. 66: Drawing by Whitman Studio. 67: Drawings by Hayward and Martin Limited. 68: Drawings by Whitman Studio. 69: Drawing by Hayward and Martin Limited—drawing by Walter Hilmers Jr.—drawing by Hayward and Martin Limited. 70–73: Drawings by Hayward and Martin Limited. 74: Drawing by Hayward and Martin Limited—drawings by John Massey. 75: Drawings by John Massey. 76–83: Drawings by Hayward and Martin Limited. 84: Drawings by Walter Hilmers Jr.—drawing by Hayward and Martin Limited. 85–87: Drawings by Hayward and Martin Limited. 88: Fil Hunter. 92: Drawing by Hayward and Martin Limited. 93, 94: Drawings by Frederic F. Bigio from B-C Graphics. 95: Drawings by Hayward and Martin Limited. 96: Drawing by Frederic F. Bigio from B-C Graphics. 97, 98: Drawings by Peter McGinn. 99: Drawings by Hayward and Martin Limited. 100: Drawings by Hayward and Martin Limited. 101: Courtesy Library of Congress. 102: John Elliott. 104: Drawings by Nick Fasciano. 105, 106: Drawings by Walter Hilmers Jr., HJ Commercial Art. 107: Drawing by Nick Fasciano—drawing by Hayward and Martin Limited. 108: Drawings by Forte Inc. 109: Drawing by Forte Inc.—drawings by Hayward and Martin Limited. 111: Drawings by Oxford Illustrators Limited. 112: Drawing by John Massey–drawings by Hayward and Martin Limited. 113–115: Drawings by Hayward and Martin Limited. 116, 117: Drawings by Peter McGinn. 119: Drawing by Whitman Studio—drawing by Hayward and Martin Limited. 120–123: Drawings by Hayward and Martin Limited.

Acknowledgements

The editors would like to thank the following: Ademco-Sontrix Ltd., Reading, Berkshire; BRK Electronics, Newbury, Berkshire; Banham Patent Locks Ltd., London; John Bishop, London Fire Brigade; Black & Decker, Dardilly, France; Wayne Boothroyd, Crime Prevention Officer, West End Central Police Station, London; Colin Bridges, London; Peter Burian Associates, London; Mr Cahill, London Fire Brigade; Kate Cann, Guildford, Surrey; Alexandra Carlier, London; Castle Alarms and Electronics, Windfield, Berkshire; C-Tec Security, Wigan, Lancashire; The Disabled Living Foundation, London; Tim Fraser, Sydney; Dan Good, Sydney; David Haviland, Hassocks, West Sussex; Liz Hodgson, London; Hoover Home Security Division, Greenford, Middlesex; Harvey Hubbell Ltd., Kempston, Bedfordshire; Anne Loch, London; John Man, Oxford; Minder Products, London; Vic Morris, ESAB, Waltham Cross, Hertfordshire; Philips Service, Croydon, Surrey; Polycell Home Security, Welwyn Garden City, Hertfordshire; Vicki Robinson, London; Warren Rogan, Sydney; Royal National Institute for the Blind, London; Inspector Snoad, Crime Prevention Section, Scotland Yard, London; Superswitch Electric Appliances Ltd., Camberley, Surrey; Mike Underhill, G.A. Collinson Fencing Co., Basildon, Essex; Weyrad Electronics Ltd., Weymouth, Dorset; Inspector Wilkinson, Crime Prevention Branch, Scotland Yard, London; Woodfit Ltd., Chorley, Lancashire; Barbara Woodhouse, London.

Index/Glossary

Included in this index are definitions of some of the typical terms used in this book. Page references in italics indicate an illustration of the subject mentioned.

Acid etching kit (for car windows), 86
Alarms, *see* Burglar alarm systems; Cars, alarm systems for; Smoke detector
Anchor: *fixing for masonry walls*; expanding, 54, *55*; hollow-wall, *55*; threaded nut, *55*; toggle, *55*
Arc welding, *see* Welding, electric arc

Basement: building strong room in , *45*; grille for windows in, 46, *54*; stairs to, 110
Bathroom: adapting for the disabled, 118, *119*, *120*; installing grab rail in, 108, *109*, *120*; laying grip strips in bath or shower, *108–109*
Battery, dry cell, 84; inserting in control box, *85*
Battery charger, 84, *85*
Bead: *strip of molten metal that hardens to secure a welded joint*; judging a, *49*; running a, 46, *48*
Bell, alarm, 57, 80; installing, *80–81*
Blind, the: safety precautions for, 103
Bolt: expanding masonry, 18, *20*; sleeve, *19*
Bolt knob, 22
Bolt lock: for casement window, *39*; installing hinge bolt, 22, *24*, *37*; installing pressbolt, 22, *25*; installing security bolt, 22, *24*, *35–36*
Burglar alarm systems, 57; central alarm system, *62–63*; closed sensor circuit, 62, *65*; control box, 62, *66*, *84–85*; door-chain alarm, *58*; false activation of, 58, *60*; fitting foil strips to windows, 62, 72, *74–75*; installing external bells and lights, 57, *80–81*; installing junction box, *76*; installing panic button, *79*; installing pressure mat, *64*, *71*, 72, *77*; internal alarm, 80; key-switched door alarm, *59*; magnetic sensor, *65*, 72; mounting magnetic sensor, *73*; open sensor circuit, 62, *64*; passive infra-red detector, 58, *62*, 66, 72, *78*; portable door alarm, *59*; routing cable, 66, *67–71*; strobe lighting, *63*, *80–81*; tamper device, 57, 62, *76*, 80, 84; telephone dialler, *81*; testing, 72, *81*; ultrasonic motion detector, 58, *60*; vibration detector, 62, 66, 72, *76*
Bypass locks and switches: *components of a burglar alarm system that allow entry to a protected area without having to switch off the complete system*; *63*, 82; cable for, 66; installing, *82*, *83*

Cabinets: childproofing, *116*, 117; fire-resistant filing, *41*; steel security, 40, *41*
Cable: chasing channel for, *69*; colour code for, 72; concealing behind skirting boards, *69*; concealing in solid wall, 66, *69*; concealing under carpet, *69*; estimating amount needed, 66; running along soil stack, *68*; running through cupboard, 66, *68*; running through stud wall, *67*; running under floorboards, *70*; size for alarms and sensors, 62, 66; threading through stair nosing, *71*
Cars: alarm systems for, 86; anti-theft devices, 86; installing ultrasonic alarm in, *86–87*
Ceilings: flame-spread ratings of, 91; installing sprinkler system in, *96*
Chain, door, 18; alarm for, *58*
Chain-link fencing, *see* Fence, chain-link
Children and safety: building fences, 103, 104; childproofing cabinets, *116*, *117*; installing fire cradle, *99*; installing stair gate, *115*
Christmas trees, flame-proofing, 91
Compass saw: using, *93*
Conduit, plastic, *16*; securing, *16*
Continuity tester: *device for finding circuit breaks*; 72
Control box (to central alarm system), 62; batteries for, 84; and colour coding, 84; connecting alarm to, *85*; hanging, *66*; locating, 62; testing, *85*; wiring circuits for, *84*; wiring connector strips to, *84*
Cradle, fire, *99*; installing, *99*
Cupboard: adapting for the disabled, *119*, *120*; childproofing, *116*, *117*; running cable through, 66, *68*
Cylinder lock: *lock operated by a grooved and notched key that engages an inner mechanism of pins and springs within cylinders*; 22, *23*; installing, *30–31*; replacing cylinder in, 26, *27*

"Dead" air space, *61*
Deadlatch rim lock: *cylinder lock mounted on inside door face with a latch that is automatically deadlocked when the door is closed*; 22, *23*
Deadlock: *lock whose bolt can be withdrawn only by turning a key*; 22; mortise, 22, *23*

"Differs", 22
Disabled, adaptations for the: in bathroom, 118, *119*, *120*; in kitchen, *120*; installing wheelchair ramp for, 118, *121–123*
Dog: electronic, 59; guard, 59
Doors: burglar alarms for, *58*, *59*; cladding with asbestos-free sheets, 92, *95*; fire-resistant, 89, 90; fitting automatic closer to, *95*; fitting limiter to, *19*; fitting magnetic sensor on, 72, *73*; fitting plasterboard round, *93*; fitting security plate to, *19*; fixing hinge to, 18, *19*; hollow-core, 18; installing bypass switch and lock to, *82*, *83*; installing intumescent strips to, *95*; installing locks on, *see* Locks; installing wide-angle viewer in, *18*; mounting grab rail on, *118*; mounting kick plate on, *118*; positioning letter box on, 18; protecting strike plate, 18, *20*; reinforcing with metal cladding, 18, *21*; securing frame, 18, *20*
Drawers: installing recessed lock in, 116, *117*
Dry chemical extinguisher, 89, *97*
Dual screw, 38, *39*

Electric cable and wire: colour coding, *16*, *17*
Electrical installations, regulations for, 14
Electrodes (for arc welders), 46, *47*
Extinguisher, *see* Fire extinguisher

Fabric, flame-proofing, 90, 91
Fence, chain-link, *8*; anatomy of, *8*; attaching winding brackets to, *11*; attaching wire mesh to, *12*; bracing posts for, *9*; digging post holes for, *9*; fixing stretcher bars to, *12*; hanging gate, *10*; installing double gates, *13*; marking post holes for, *9*; ordering materials for, 8; regulations regarding, 8; setting post in concrete for, *10*; splicing wire-mesh rolls, *13*; straining line wire, *11*
Fence, wooden: building regulations regarding, 104; hanging gate, *106*; hanging rails, *105*; making gate, *106*; placing gateposts, 104; setting posts, *104*; spacing boards, *105*; stepping down slope, *107*
Filing cabinet, fire-resistant, *41*
Fire: causes of, 89, 90; classes of, 97; deaths from, 7; exit routes in case of, *99*, *100*; flame-spread rating of building materials, 91; how to put out, 97, 100

(*see also* Fire extinguisher); installing smoke detector, 58, *61*; making door fire-resistant, 92, *95*; protecting furniture from, 90, *91*; protecting valuables from, 40, *41*; protecting walls and ceilings against, 90, 92, *93–94*; safety check list, 90; treating timber floor against, *92*

Fire drill, *100*
Fire escape: ladder, *99*; sling and cradle, *99*
Fire extinguisher: advantages and limitations of, 98; carbon dioxide, *97*, 98; dry chemical, *89*, *97*, 98; foam, *97*; locating, 97; operating, *98*; sprinkler system, *96*; vapourizing liquid, *97*; water, *97*, 98
Fire fighting, professional, 101
Fire-retardant solutions, 90; mixing and applying, *91*; recipes for, 91
Flame-spread ratings, 91
"Flashover", 101
Floors: bolting safe to, *43*; laying cable under, *70*; making fire-resistant, 90, *92*. *See also* Pressure mat
Fluorescent lamps, 14. *See also* Lighting, security
Flux, 46
Foil strip, *62*, *72*; attaching, *74–75*; installing connector blocks for, *75*
Forest fires, 90
French windows: installing security bolt on, 22, *24*, *35–36*
Furnishings: making flame-resistant, 90, *91*

Garages: magnetic sensors for, *63*, *72*, *74*; padlocks and hasps for, 22, *25*; smoke detectors in, 61
Gate, safety: installing on stairs, *115*
Gates: aligning hanging and slamming posts, *10*, *104*; installing double, *13*; installing thumb latch on, *106*; making wooden, *106*
Glass doors, *see* French windows
Grab rail, 108; installing in bath or shower, *109*, 118, *119*, *120*; mounting on door, *118*
Grille, window, *7*; anchors for, 54, *55*; installing in reveal, *54*, *55*; making jig for, *51*, *52*; ornamental, 46, *52–53*; pickets, 46; sliding, 46; spreaders, 46; types of, 46; welding basic grille, 46, 51. *See also* Welding, electric arc
Grip strips, 108; for stairs, 110; laying in

bath or shower, *108–109*; laying in front of sink or washing machine, *108*
Gypsum plasterboard, *see* Plasterboard

Handrail, stair, *103*, 110; installing, *111–115*; joining sections of, 110; positioning brackets for, *111*; securing brackets for, *112*
Hasp, *see* Padlock
Hasp lock: *lock for cabinet doors*; 116; installing, *117*
Head plate: *horizontal top member of a timber-frame wall*; drilling through, *67*
Hinge bolt, 22, *24*; installing, *37*
Hinge, door, 18; deep fixing for, *19*

Incandescent lamps, 14. *See also* Lighting, security
Insurance companies: and external grilles, 54; and safes, 40
Intrusion alarm, 58; door-chain, *58*; key-switched, *59*; portable, *59*; ultrasonic motion detector, 58, *60*. *See also* Passive infra-red detector
Intumescent paint, 90
Intumescent strips, installing, 92, *95*

Jig: *clamp for holding a workpiece or guiding a tool*; making for grilles, *51*, *52*
Joint box: connecting, *17*; positioning, 14
Jumper wires: *wires used to connect adjacent terminals*; *84*
Junction box: installing, *76*

Kick plate: attaching to door, *118*
Kitchen: adapting for wheelchair, 118, *120*; and causes of fire, 90; laying grip strips in, *108–109*

Ladder, emergency, 99; installing, *99*
Lamp, *see* Lighting, security
LED, *see* Light-emitting diode
Lever lock: *lock operated by a flat-bitted key that engages an inner mechanism of levers and springs*; 22, 26
Light-emitting diode, 72, 76, 78
Lighting, security: connecting joint box for, 17; fixing backplate for, 16; fixing cable conduit for, 16; fluorescent lamps, 14; incandescent lamps, 14, 15; installing manual switch for, 17; installing photocell for, 14, 15; installing supply cable for, 16; mercury vapour lamps, 14; mounting on outside wall, *16–17*; positioning joint box for, 14; positioning

of, 14, *15*; sodium lamps, 14, *15*; tungsten halogen lamps, 14; types of lamp fixtures, 15. *See also* Strobe light
Limiter, door: fitting, *19*
Line wires, 8; straining, *11*
Locks: anatomy of, 22; attaching showcase, *116*; cylinder, 22; deadlatch rim, *23*; deadlock, 22, 23; five-lever mortise deadlock, 22, *23*; for sliding door, 22, *25*; for window, 38, *39*; hasp lock, 116; installing hasp lock, *117*; installing mortised multipoint, *32–34*; installing mortised sash lock, *30–31*; installing recessed drawer lock, *117*; installing rim lock, 26, *28–29*; multipoint, 22, *24*; padlocks and hasps, 22, *25*; protection for strike plate, 18, *20*; recessed drawer lock, 116; replacing cylinder, 26, *27*; sash, 22, *23*; showcase, 116; springlatch rim, 22, *23*, 26. *See also* Bolt locks

Magnetic sensor: *intrusion detector that triggers an alarm when magnetic contact between two parts of a switch is broken*; *62–63*; anodized, 72; installing bypass switch for, *82*; mounting on window, *73*; recessed, 72; recessing for door, *73*; surface-mounted, 72; wiring for, *65*
Mercury vapour lamps, 14. *See* Lighting, security
Mortise deadlock: *key-operated lock housed in the closing edge of a door*; 22, *23*; installing, 26, *30–31*; installing multipoint, *32–34*
Motion detector, 58, *63*, 72; for safes and strong rooms, 40, *45*; testing, 72; ultrasonic, 58, *60*
"Mouse": using a, *67*, *68*
Multipoint lock: *high-security lock with two or more bolts*; 22, *24*; installing, *32–34*

Newel post: *structural vertical member of a staircase balustrade*; securing when loose, 110, *111*
Nightlatch, *see* Springlatch
Noggings: *bracing timbers between wall studs*; 67
Nosing: *rounded front edge of a stair tread*; threading cable through, *71*

Padlocks and hasps, 22, *25*
Panic button: *button wired to a continuous circuit that can set off an alarm when all other parts of a system are switched off*;

62, 63, 72; attaching mounting box for, 79; connecting up, 79

Passive infra-red detector: *detector that triggers an alarm in response to changes in infra-red energy*; 58, 62; cable for, 66; positioning of, 72, 78; wiring for, 78

Patio door: installing magnetic sensor for, 72, 73; lock for, 22, 25

Photocell, 14, 15

Pickets, 46; twisting, 52; welding to spreaders, 51

PIR, *see* Passive infra-red detector

Plasterboard, gypsum, 91, 92; attaching to wall, 93; fitting round door, 93; fitting round pipes and ducts, 94

Poisoning: deaths from, 7; prevention of, 103

Pope, Alexander, 57

Pressbolt, 22, 25

Pressure mat, 62, 64; laying, 77; positioning, 40, 45, 72; running cable for, 66; testing, 72; wiring for, 64; wiring for on stairs, 71

Ramp, wheelchair: dimensions of, 118; fixing handrails to, 123; installing, 121–123; materials for, 118

Ramp-piece: *angled section of handrail at staircase top*; 110, 112–115

Reed switch, 65

Rim lock: *lock mounted on the inside face of a door*; deadlatch, 23; installing, 26, 28–29; springlatch, 22, 23, 26

Safes: bolting to floor, 43; building false wall for, 42; burglary-resistant, 40, 41; encasing in concrete blocks, 44; fire-resistant, 40, 41; in-floor, 40, 41; installing in wall, 42–43; and insurance companies, 40; moving, 40; positioning of, 40

Sash lock: *lock combining key-operated bolt with handle-operated latch*; 22, 23; installing, 30–31

Sash stop: *sash window lock that prevents sashes from being fully opened*; 38; installing, 39

Screw, non-retractable: fitting, 38

Security bolt, 22, 24; installing on French windows, 24, 35–36

Security plate: fitting, 19

Sensor: closed-circuit, 64, 65; installing junction box for, 76; open-circuit, 64

Showcase lock: *lock for cabinet with sliding glass doors*; 116; attaching, 116

Shower: adapting for wheelchair, 118, 119; installing grab rail in, 109; laying grip strips on floor of, 108–109

Shunt keep: *box-type strike plate containing a bypass switch*; 63, 82; cable for, 66, 82; installing, 83

Shunt mortise lock: *mortise lock incorporating a bypass switch*; 82; cable for, 66, 82; installing, 83

Siren, alarm, 63, 80; installing, 80–81

Slag, 46; removing, 48, 49

Sleeve bolt: *two-piece bolt with smooth, convex exposed end*; using, 19, 21

Sling, fire, 99; installing, 99

Smoke detector, 58; ionization, 61; locating in house, 61; locating in room, 61; photo-electric, 61; and safes and strong rooms, 40, 45; testing, 61

Sodium lamps: high-pressure, 14, 15; low-pressure, 14; with flood lens, 15. *See* Lighting, security

Soffit: *underside of edge of roof*; 16

Soldering connections, 77

Spreaders, 46; extended, 54; welding to pickets, 51

Springlatch rim lock: *cylinder lock mounted on inside door face and operated by a key from outside and a knob from inside*; 22, 23, 26

Sprinkler system, 96, 96

Stairs: badly designed, 110; carpeting for, 110; grip strips for, 110; installing handrail for, 103, 110, 111–115; installing pressure mat on, 71; installing safety gate on, 115; securing loose newel post, 110, 111

Steering lock, car, 86

Stile: *vertical framing member of a door*; strengthening, 19

Straining posts, 8; setting up, 9–10

Stretcher bar, 8; fixing, 12

Strike box: *box mounted on doorframe to receive a rim lock bolt or latch*; 18; reinforcement bar for, 20; securing, 32

Strike plate: *metal plate secured to door-jamb with holes to receive a mortise lock bolt or latch*; 18; reinforcement bar for, 20

Strobe light, 63, 80; attaching to alarm box, 80; linking with alarm, 80–81

Strong room, building a, 45

Tack welding, 50

Tamper circuit, 57, 62, 76, 80; colour coding, 84

Telephone dialler, automatic, 81

Television: and fire hazards, 90

Thumb latch: installing, 106

Toggle anchor: *fixing for hollow walls or concrete blocks*; 55

Trunking, PVC: *cable conduit with rectangular cross-section*; 66; using, 70

Tungsten halogen lamps, 14

Ultrasonic alarm, 86; installing in car, 86–87

Ultrasonic motion detector: *detector that triggers an alarm in response to disturbance in a pattern of high-frequency sound waves*; 58, 60; positioning, 60

Upholstery: making fire-resistant, 90, 91; putting out fire in, 97

Vibration detector, 62, 72; cable for, 66; installing, 76; testing, 72

Viewer, wide-angle: installing, 18

Walls: adding plasterboard layer to, 92, 93–94; attaching grille to, 54, 55; concealing cable in, 66, 67, 69; flame-spread ratings of, 91; mounting light on, 16–17

Wardrobe: adapting for disabled person, 119

Watson, Thomas, 57

Welder, arc: anatomy of, 47; electrodes for, 46, 47; using, *see* Welding, electric arc

Welding, electric arc, 7, 46; butt joint, 50; fillet joint, 50; flux for, 46; forming a scroll, 53; judging a bead, 49; making a circle, 52; making a diamond, 52; making a simple grille, 46, 51; removing slag, 48, 49; running a bead, 46, 48; safety precautions, 46, 47; striking an arc, 48; tacking a joint, 50

Welding, gas, 46

Wheelchair: adapting bathroom for, 120; adapting door for, 118; adapting kitchen for, 118, 120; adapting shower for, 118, 119; installing ramp for, 118, 121–123

Wheel nuts, anti-theft, 86

Winding bracket, 8; attaching, 11

Windows: alarm systems for, 58, 59; installing emergency ladder, 99; installing foil strip alarm, 72, 74–75; installing grille on, 46, 51–55 (*see also* Welding); installing sling or cradle, 99; locks for, 38, 39; mounting magnetic sensor on, 72, 73

Wire-mesh fencing, *see* Fence, chain-link

Metric Conversion Chart

Approximate equivalents—length

Millimetres to inches		Inches to millimetres	
1	1/32	1/32	1
2	1/16	1/16	2
3	1/8	1/8	3
4	5/32	3/16	5
5	3/16	1/4	6
6	1/4	5/16	8
7	9/32	3/8	10
8	5/16	7/16	11
9	11/32	1/2	13
10 (1cm)	3/8	9/16	14
11	7/16	5/8	16
12	15/32	11/16	17
13	1/2	3/4	19
14	9/16	13/16	21
15	19/32	7/8	22
16	5/8	15/16	24
17	11/16	1	25
18	23/32	2	51
19	3/4	3	76
20	25/32	4	102
25	1	5	127
30	1 3/16	6	152
40	1 9/16	7	178
50	1 31/32	8	203
60	2 3/8	9	229
70	2 3/4	10	254
80	3 5/32	11	279
90	3 9/16	12 (1ft)	305
100	3 15/16	13	330
200	7 7/8	14	356
300	11 13/16	15	381
400	15 3/4	16	406
500	19 11/16	17	432
600	23 3/8	18	457
700	27 9/16	19	483
800	31 1/2	20	508
900	35 7/16	24 (2ft)	610
1000 (1m)	39 3/8		

Metres to feet/inches		Yards to metres	
		1	0.914
2	6' 7"	2	1.83
3	9' 10"	3	2.74
4	13' 1"	4	3.66
5	16' 5"	5	4.57
6	19' 8"	6	5.49
7	23' 0"	7	6.40
8	26' 3"	8	7.32
9	29' 6"	9	8.23
10	32' 10"	10	9.14
20	65' 7"	20	18.29
50	164' 0"	50	45.72
100	328' 1"	100	91.44

Conversion factors

Length	1 millimetre (mm)	= 0.0394 in
	1 centimetre (cm)/10 mm	= 0.3937 in
	1 metre/100 cm	= 39.37 in/3.281 ft/1.094 yd
	1 kilometre (km)/1000 metres	= 1093.6 yd/0.6214 mile
	1 inch (in)	= 25.4 mm/2.54 cm
	1 foot (ft)/12 in	= 304.8 mm/30.48 cm/0.3048 metre
	1 yard (yd)/3 ft	= 914.4 mm/91.44 cm/0.9144 metre
	1 mile/1760 yd	= 1609.344 metres/1.609 km
Area	1 square centimetre (sq cm)/ 100 square millimetres (sq mm)	= 0.155 sq in
	1 square metre (sq metre)/10,000 sq cm	= 10.764 sq ft/1.196 sq yd
	1 are/100 sq metres	= 119.60 sq yd/0.0247 acre
	1 hectare (ha)/100 ares	= 2.471 acres/0.00386 sq mile
	1 square inch (sq in)	= 645.16 sq mm/6.4516 sq cm
	1 square foot (sq ft)/144 sq in	= 929.03 sq cm
	1 square yard (sq yd)/9 sq ft	= 8361.3 sq cm/0.8361 sq metre
	1 acre/4840 sq yd	= 4046.9 sq metres/0.4047 ha
	1 square mile/640 acres	= 259 ha/2.59 sq km
Volume	1 cubic centimetre (cu cm)/ 1000 cubic millimetres (cu mm)	= 0.0610 cu in
	1 cubic decimetre (cu dm)/1000 cu cm	= 61.024 cu in/0.0353 cu ft
	1 cubic metre/1000 cu dm	= 35.3147 cu ft/1.308 cu yd
	1 cu cm	= 1 millilitre (ml)
	1 cu dm	= 1 litre see **Capacity**
	1 cubic inch (cu in)	= 16.3871 cu cm
	1 cubic foot (cu ft)/1728 cu in	= 28,316.8 cu cm/0·0283 cu metre
	1 cubic yard (cu yd)/27 cu ft	= 0.7646 cu metre
Capacity	1 litre	= 1.7598 pt/0.8799 qt/0.22 gal
	1 pint (pt)	= 0.568 litre
	1 quart (qt)	= 1.137 litres
	1 gallon (gal)	= 4.546 litres
Weight	1 gram (g)	= 0.035 oz
	1 kilogram (kg)/1000 g	= 2.20 lb/35.2 oz
	1 tonne/1000 kg	= 2204.6 lb/0.9842 ton
	1 ounce (oz)	= 28.35 g
	1 pound (lb)	= 0.4536 kg
	1 ton	= 1016 kg
Pressure	1 gram per square metre (g/metre^2)	= 0.0295 oz/sq yd
	1 gram per square centimetre (g/cm^2)	= 0.228 oz/sq in
	1 kilogram per square centimetre (kg/cm^2)	= 14.223 lb/sq in
	1 kilogram per square metre (kg/metre^2)	= 0.205 lb/sq ft
	1 pound per square foot (lb/ft^2)	= 4.882 kg/metre^2
	1 pound per square inch (lb/in^2)	= 703.07 kg/metre^2
	1 ounce per square yard (oz/yd^2)	= 33.91 g/metre^2
	1 ounce per square foot (oz/ft^2)	= 305.15 g/metre^2
Temperature	To convert °F to °C, subtract 32, then divide by 9 and multiply by 5	
	To convert °C to °F, divide by 5 and multiply by 9, then add 32	

Phototypeset by Tradespools Limited, Frome, Somerset
Colour reproduction by Grafascan Limited
Printed and bound by Artes Gráficas, Toledo, SA, Spain

D. L. TO: 481-1986